THE Rainbow YEARS

THE *Rainbow* YEARS

RACHEL VIVIEN

Once upon a time . . . all good stories start like this. This is the story of a missionary child born in 1941 to Kenneth and Wendy Moynagh.

RACHEL

Wendy Martin-Harvey was the youngest of four children – Doris, Gwen, Martin and Wendy. They lived in a big house built by Wendy's father, Thomas, when he got a promotion. He was clever. He went to work for a firm called British Calendar and Cables. He was 16 and made the tea. Then he had a good idea and got promoted. By the time Wendy was born, he had enough money to live in a house with a tennis court and have a chauffeur called Wallington – well Wallington was the chauffeur when I was born.

Wendy's mother was a good Christian lady who ran a Sunday school class once a week in her drawing room – it was a posh house so the sitting room was called a drawing room. She was a shy lady so when her husband was asked to be Mayor of London, he refused because he knew his wife, May, my granny, would never manage dressing up and talking to people. All the children went to private schools.

Doris was good at acting. She went to The Royal Academy of Dance and Drama and was called the Tragedy Queen. She was hauled off the stage by her parents before she was called a Loose Woman as that would have been a tragedy! She decided to join a Christian organisation that had camps for girls and off she went with her mother in tow to do the cooking – not quite the same as being the wife of the Mayor of London!

Gwen skipped school as often as she could but when her father realised what was going on, he went to the school gates at the end of the school day to meet Gwen who wasn't there. He was a wise father so he told his wayward daughter that he had been to meet her after school and was disappointed to have missed her! She didn't risk it again. When Doris decided she had better have some training in being a good Christian she signed up for a two-year course at Ridgelands Bible College; Gwen thought she had better tow the party line so she signed up too.

Wendy liked school. She played tennis in the school team, kept her head down and worked hard. When she left school she went to London to do a cookery course and learn how to be a good housewife – flower arranging and that sort of thing. Then she met a handsome doctor that Gwen knew and liked a lot. He preferred Wendy – Wendy kept very quiet about that! He was at St Barts hospital and as Wendy wanted to be a physiotherapist, she decided to go there too. They both thought this was a good idea. Then Wendy had cold feet. Did she just want to be a physiotherapist because John was at Barts and what if Gwen found out? Maybe God wanted her at Ridgelands Bible College too? It was certainly a safer bet. Off she went to college, John got forgotten about and Gwen, blissfully unaware of her little sister's love life, hankered after John until her dying day – yes she really did!

Here is an aside: many years later when Gwen had married Raymond and, in their eighties, they went to South Africa on holiday, they went to church on a Sunday. Who should be playing the organ but John! Gwen was quite bowled over, couldn't listen to any of the service and whispered to Raymond, "The man playing the organ is the John I have loved since I was a teenager!" Then Raymond couldn't listen to the service either. When John had played the last note on the organ Gwen told Raymond he would have to find his own way back to the place where they were staying because she was going back with John in his car and was going to have a private conversation. As always, Raymond did as he was told. Gwen never divulged the private conversation but that was the last time she saw John.

When Wendy finished at Bible College, the war had broken out and so she went to Plymouth to help in a Sailors' Rest which was a house where troops on leave, with nowhere better to go, had meetings and meals. Gwen went to work in her father's factory in Slough, looking after the welfare of the women who worked in the factory. Doris worked as a Good Christian doing Good Christian Things.

Kenneth Moynagh was born in Kenya. His father had emigrated as a young man with little prospects of a decent life in England and an entrepreneurial streak. He did well as a trader in whatever was available and bought up a considerable amount of land. He met a pretty Irish nurse who had left Ireland when she felt the call to be a missionary and convert the heathen in Kenya. Kenneth's father turned out to be the heathen that needed converting! She married him and set about the task. They had four children – Digby, Kenneth, Eileen and Alan. But converting that particular heathen proved too much and she left him and went back to England taking the children with her. He met another lady who had no interest in his soul. They had lots of parties, used up all the money, sold the land for a pittance – needs must – and went to South Africa. His ex-wife managed a nursing home in Epsom, and was as poor as a church mouse but did get grants to send her three sons to Epsom College.

Digby and Alan went to London hospitals to train as doctors; Digby to Barts and Alan to St. Mary's. Kenneth wanted to do the same and got a place at Barts subject to interview. On the day of the interview, his mother told him there was no money to pay his fees and he was to go and tell them to cancel his place. As he set off he passed the postman. Before he got to the corner of the road his mother called him back. An envelope had arrived with enough money to allow him to go after all. "God provides," his mother told him. He went to Barts, played rugby for the hospital and was invited to the Christian Union which changed his life. He had always been to church with his mother but this demanded something far more – a personal commitment to a God who would make demands but not without the strength to meet those demands.

He joined The Sudan Missionary Society which supported him through his training but it folded up after the war so he had to apply to a different mission. He was most of the way through his training when the war broke out and he signed up to join the army as a medical officer. He did not talk about the war. He went to France and was rescued at Dunkirk. He was shipped back to Plymouth and, at a loose end, he went to a Bible Study meeting at the Sailor's Rest. Wendy was on duty that evening. She made him tea, gave him a hymn book, played the piano for the singing and fluttered her eyelashes at the handsome young man with a ginger moustache.

Love at first sight was convenient in the war as time was at a premium. They got engaged six weeks later and Wendy took Kenneth home to meet her parents and for him to ask her father's permission to marry his youngest daughter. Her father sized him up and gave them his blessing. Her mother was unsure – his background was unsavoury, his father had been a travelling musician and jack-of-all-trades, but Kenneth had a good profession and was able to provide for Wendy. They were married on February 1st 1941. Her wedding dress was made out of parachute silk. They lived in a cottage in Tiverton, Devon. Wendy had a maid to help with the chores. By the spring she knew for certain she was pregnant and I was born in Exeter Hospital on December 23rd 1941. Gwen jumped on a train and was the first to welcome her niece into the strange new world she would occupy for a very long time.

Me, aged 18 months

TOMATIN

Kenneth spent three months with his new daughter and then packed his bags and went to West Africa. Wendy soldiered on for three more months and then dismissed the maid and went back home to the safety of Tomatin and settled down with her parents and Gwen.

My grandparents house called 'Tomatin'

My grandfather was commuting between London and Slough where there was a large factory making cables for telephone and telegraph systems. Gwen went to work in the factory looking after the interests of the women who worked there. My grandmother battened down the hatches at home – until the war effort demanded that homes should be opened up to evacuees. Gwen left the factory to help at home – Granny could not be expected to wash out the lice which crawled about the evacuees' hair, let alone make all the beds and do all the cooking without another pair of hands. Maids had left to do more appropriate war work but Arnold, the odd job man, had stayed to hold the fort. He was too old to sign up for the army and Mrs Arnold had a sharp tongue on her so best be out of the house as much as possible. My mother and I settled in, helping with the running of the house, organising the evacuees and waiting for letters from West Africa. Kenneth's long-awaited Leave was cancelled and a letter came telling Wendy that he had visited Uncle Walter. Uncle Walter lived in India so Wendy gulped back her tears, gave me a hug and explained that Daddy wasn't coming home after all and they would have to wait. That didn't worry me at all. I had no idea who "daddy" was and was quite content to be just the five of us, plus Arnold and Twinkle, the cat.

The rhythm of the days was, in its way, healing. Time slipped by. In the summer I helped my Grandfather pick the fruit from the raspberry, currant and gooseberry bushes.

In my grandparents garden

Granny made jam and bottled apples, pears and peaches. She used Kilner jars to preserve the fruit – peaches from the tree on the south wall of the house, plums from the plum tree and slices of apple from the apple trees. She made jam from raspberries from the canes in the vegetable garden and gooseberries from the prickly gooseberry bushes. There were expeditions to a local strawberry farm where the grown-ups picked baskets of strawberries and I ate the big, juicy red ones when nobody was looking. A red mouth was an unfortunate giveaway! Aunty Gwen kept hens and I helped collect the eggs – until one of the hens pecked my toes and then I felt it was much more appropriate to supervise from a safe distance. Aunty Gwen kept bees, two hives, and I dressed up in a hat with a net over my face, one of my Grandfather's shirts tied tightly at the wrists, gloves, my pyjama trousers and Wellington boots. I was still terrified; the bees buzzed right by my ears. I helped Aunty Gwen lift off the trays full of dripping honeycombs. The bees buzzed about but they couldn't get past The defences and I loved pouring in the sugar solution to help them make their honey – until sugar rationing put a stop to that and the bees had to fend for themselves. There was a vegetable garden too with peas and beans climbing up their poles and lots and lots of horrible cabbages which both Mummy and Aunty Gwen told me were good for me. Butter was in short supply so Grandpa, lovingly nick-named Gaga, told me to turn over my bread so that I would be able to taste it. Aunty Gwen made "good for you" brown bread and I learnt to eat up everything because there were lots of people who didn't have as much as I did. I suggested posting the cabbage to them but nobody took any notice. At Christmas Granny made a Christmas cake. I was allowed to help as long as I didn't get in the way. Aunty Gwen found bowls and bags of ingredients and then I got out of the way while Granny set to. She had to sieve currants, raisins and sultanas to get the weevils out. She put them in the sieve, covered them with a sprinkling of flour and shook the sieve until all the flour and the weevils fell out into the bowl underneath. When they were all out, she threw away the weevilly flour and made a Christmas cake with all the saved-up sugar and butter and everyone agreed it had been worth going without butter and sugar because the cake was so delicious. I was allowed to scrape out the bowl. I sat on the stool with a tea towel around my neck and used my fingers to get out every last bit of the mixture. "What a luxury!" everyone said – everyone except me; I liked sugar on my porridge for breakfast and butter on my toast and didn't like Christmas cake – except for the scrapings out of the bowl. Once a year my Grandfather went up to London for a special, important dinner and came back with a surprise. A tangerine and a BANANA! The only knowledge I had of bananas was from a picture book. The real banana brought back from London had to be shared between the five of us. My little bit was delicious.

Aunty Doris visited from London where she lived with Uncle Oliver and their son, Mervyn. Grandpa didn't think Uncle Oliver was good enough for Aunty Doris so he paid a lot of money so that Oliver could work at Lloyds Insurance and have a nice house. They had Nanny to look after Mervyn, and Brian and Denham when they were born later on, and Molly to do everything else while Aunty Doris went on doing the Lord's work and speaking at meetings. Uncle Oliver looked after Aunty Doris very well – he had to with his father-in-law keeping an eye on him. He cleaned her shoes and ran her bath for her and at half past nine every night of their married life he put on the kettle and made a cup of tea. Visitors knew then that it was time for Aunty Doris to go to bed! Everyone else went to bed too. In the winter it was Christmas with a tree and going to the circus on Boxing Day. I liked the elephants and the trapeze artists but not the clowns. I didn't think they were at all funny and when they hopped over the barrier I hid under the seat. I was terrified of their big lips and shiny noses. I loved those Christmas visits with the table opened up as big as it would go and Molly's constant reprimands," No, Miss Rachel, you mustn't keep on picking. You won't want a proper meal." Nanny seemed to do all the cooking with Aunty Doris taking credit for it. I was never brave enough to point out that she hadn't done anything much more than look at the turkey when Nanny pulled it out of the Aga oven! They were halcyon days for me untouched by the war.

When the weather improved, Aunty Gwen went horse riding. The horse came to the gate and Aunty Gwen dressed up in her special riding breeches, Boots and hat and off she went. She didn't ride out on Hunts but she did run with the hounds when the Hunt was on foot and came home very dirty and with a red face. She took me up the road to feed the horses in the field. I was instructed to put an apple on my hand and keep my hand flat so that the horse would eat the apple and not my fingers. It was all very frightening but the horse did like the apple. One day we went up the road not to visit the horse but to see where a bomb had fallen and left a big hole. I thought the hole was so big it would take only a few digs to get to Australia – Aunty Gwen had told me that if we dug far enough in the vegetable garden we would get to Australia - so I sensibly suggested we went back and got our spades and had a go but Aunty Gwen said it was lunchtime and we had better go home.

When Aunty Gwen was busy Mrs Arnold took me for walks in my pushchair – "I can't be doin' with dawdlin'!" said Mrs Arnold. Mrs Arnold told me she couldn't abide the colour red so whenever we passed a red gate I said," Look at that gate," and Mrs Arnold said," Oh, Miss Rachel, you are a tease!" and then we both laughed – until Mrs Arnold got fed up and said, "That's enough now!" in a voice that said it really was enough. One day we all dressed up in our best clothes – I wore a blue coat with a velvet collar – because Uncle Martin had won a medal and we all had a photo taken in the front garden. That was before a bomb landed in the hedge. Luckily it didn't go off and the bomb disposal people came and took it away.

Picking fruit with Arnold

At night time my mother and I shared a room. Every night my mother put combs in her hair to keep in the waves, no curls, and tied a hair net over them. When the siren went off I woke up and hurried Mummy ahead of me down into the shelter. It had a light bulb which didn't give much light, beds and a chair and it smelt funny. Arnold had a room in the house and he said he'd rather be bombed in his bed than go into the shelter. I didn't think he liked Mrs Arnold very much because he didn't want to go home to sleep in his own bed. I did ask Arnold why he stayed with them and he said he'd rather die in his bed alone than have Mrs Arnold grumbling about "them Germans". I thought that was very sensible because sometimes, on their walks, I got a bit fed up with Mrs Arnold's grumbling. There were so many broken nights that in the end it was decided that we would all de-camp and spend every night in the shelter – except for Arnold who stayed in his bed in the house. In the mornings, he would open the shelter door and stand on the steps with the light behind him and say," Mornin' all!" and everyone was glad that they had got through another night safely.

They were very happy years for me. I was a good little girl; I could see no point in being anything but good. I knew how loved I was both by my grandparents and my beloved Aunty Gwen and I knew too that God loved me. I said my prayers every night at bedtime and I understood, as much as any three-year-old can comprehend, that I needed to "ask Jesus into my heart" and then He would always be there to listen to me and rescue me when necessary. One day, sitting on my potty in the upstairs Loo at Tomatin, I asked my mother whether this would be a good time to say this special prayer. Mummy said she thought it would be a very good time, she was sure Jesus didn't mind my being on my potty in the loo, so I told Jesus that I was ready to ask Him to share my life and I have to say I have never regretted that decision. It was a home which adhered to strict Christian principles. Church every Sunday of course but Granny also had a Sunday School in the Drawing Room every Sunday afternoon where she gathered up about 40 children and taught them Bible Stories illustrated with pictures cut out and stuck onto pieces of flannel which would stick onto a flannel-covered board. It was called Flannel-Graph. So from my earliest days, I was well grounded in Bible stories. Wendy left Gwen and her mother to their Sunday School and she climbed onto her bike and peddled off to a Crusader Class. I stood at the kitchen window and waved her off. Then I asked Aunty Gwen every half an hour when Mummy would be home again. I sensed that it was never very safe to let her out of my sight – bombs were no Respecter of Persons. Aunty Gwen made pancakes for tea and I "helped" by licking out the bowl. The last pancake was always in the shape of an R and that was the tasting one. It was delicious with a scrape of butter and a lick of jam!

Licking out the bowl!

Three years and nine months went by. During that time Kenneth had felt the call to be a missionary. He had visited a mission station in India and had been asked to come back after the war to be a missionary doctor there. He didn't feel that India was the place God wanted him but he did feel he should be a missionary in Africa. Despite being so young when he left Africa it somehow gets into your bones and Daddy was determined to go back. African heathens were much needier than Indians who seemed to have plenty of missionaries there already. He felt a sense of obligation to Africa having had so much support from the Sudan mission. He wrote to Wendy asking her if she was willing to go with him. She wrote him a strong letter saying it was out of the question. Poor Kenneth was devastated but when he talked to a lovely older missionary lady called Amy Carmichael who told him all would be well, he decided to leave well alone till he got back to England. Wendy felt really bad about her quick response and wrote another letter saying she would go with him wherever he felt was the place for them. She didn't fancy Africa at all. Her father had made a trip to Africa before the war when Gwen was out there helping a missionary doctor and his wife in Kenya. She was teaching the African children how to be Christians and not little heathens. She took out with her the Flannel-graph board and the pictures – all of the white people dressed in the most peculiar clothes, though perhaps no more peculiar than the ones the missionaries wore. Jesus must have seemed even more remote to them than He did to the children in an English Sunday School but she persisted, sitting on the grass outside in her large brimmed hat, chatting away in English which not one of them understood. They did love the pictures though if the crowds that turned up were anything to go by. It's lucky God moves in a mysterious way! Her parents had visited her there and her father had caught Black-water Fever and nearly died. He had been rushed back to England and vowed never to go back to Africa again. Wendy had no desire to risk life and limb - besides there were snakes and creepy crawly things in Africa and plenty of Heathen in England who could be preached to. On the other hand, she loved Kenneth and she hadn't seen him for three years. Could she really write to him and say no way? She prayed and prayed and told Gwen who was far more pragmatic about the whole situation. Gwen's suggestion was to write to Kenneth and tell him she wasn't very keen on the idea but they would talk it over when he got back and make a plan then. Wendy thought this was good advice. She wrote the letter and made sure she gave him plenty of news about his daughter so that he would remember there were three of them to think about and not just the two of them. Kenneth never received that letter. He waited and waited and in England, Wendy wondered why he never mentioned it again. She thought it was better to let sleeping dogs lie so she put the letter away and got on with praying that he wouldn't be killed in the meantime. On Sundays, they went to Church and prayed for Kenneth and I said Amen loudly so that God would hear, though I had no idea who I was praying for but I knew he was important to Mummy. I was a bit concerned that he was more important to her than I was but, when I told her this concern, she gave me a big hug and told me we were both very important to her which wasn't as reassuring as she hoped!

One of my favourite things was having stories read to me. Of all the books the best was "The Cuckoo Clock". The clock was owned by a Mr Knee-breeches and I loved pretending to be him. I put on Aunty Gwent's brown bloomers – in those far-off days ladies wore pants and then, for decency, they wore bloomers over them which were baggy and reached to their knees and were convenient for tucking a hanky into! They had to be tied around my knees with string. I pulled up my socks so they nearly reached my knees and I was all set, just like Mr Knee-Breeches. Aunty Gwen would pick up the phone and hold down the connection so that she could pretend to talk to Mr Knee-breeches and sometimes I talked to him too but he never answered which was disappointing though he did seem to answer Aunty Gwen – all very puzzling. You must understand that in those days the phone stood on a stand with a dial on it and you had to dial the numbers by slotting your finger into each number and turning the dial. Of course, if you held down the connection button there was no connection. But to me, it was all so real that one day it all went too far and I felt swallowed up and had to ask Aunty Gwen to help me back to being Rachel again. Aunty Gwen whipped off the bloomers, pulled down the socks and all was back to normal. I decided to keep Mr Knee-breeches in the book – he was much safer there. They were very happy days. I basked in the love that was showered on me and had no reason to be anything other than a pleasure!

I shared Aunty Gwen with my grandparents and sometimes Uncle Martin when he came home on leave from the Navy. He was a keen bird watcher and one day he nearly got arrested. He was bird-watching on the deck of his ship using his new binoculars. He was accused of being a spy! Goodness knows who accused him but he came home rather shaken by the whole adventure. I overheard the bit about being a spy which I thought was very exciting and straight out of a storybook where spies were usually the baddies! Uncle Martin was too nice to be a baddy so I was a bit bemused by the whole incident. Spy or not, he did get a medal and there is a nice photo of me with Uncle Martin and the medal, standing by the hedge in the front garden at Tomatin. I am wearing my best blue coat with a velvet collar.

And then the war came to an end and one day the phone rang. Daddy was home. Mummy smiled and smiled. Her father booked a room at the Dorchester Hotel in London and Mummy packed a case, kissed me goodbye and jumped on the train. I wanted to go too and cried but Aunty Gwen scooped me up and suggested phoning Mr Knee-breeches and telling him the exciting news – Daddy was home at last. I think it was then that I first suspected I was not going to be the centre of Mummy's world any more; change was in the air and I didn't like it.

Daddy's return

ALL CHANGE

The next day everyone got busy changing things in the house. I was moved out of the room I had been sharing with my mother – "No, darling, you can't stay in that room because Mummy and Daddy need to be together so you can have your own room." – and a bed was put up in my grandfather's dressing room. I protested loudly, it was worse than I had anticipated, but the "No" was not going to change to "Yes" so I gave up. This was to be the first of many changes.

When the front doorbell rang, I was the first one there I couldn't wait to see Mummy back again safely. Aunty Gwen opened the door and there was Mummy and a huge big Man. "Hallo Rachel", he said. He was very big and I was aware for the first time, that I was quite small – well I was growing but not very fast – so I waited till Mummy picked me up before I said "Hallo" back. He could come in for a little while as long as he left soon so I could talk to Mummy properly. But he had come to stay and had brought three presents – a doll nearly as big as me with black hair and staring eyes. I was terrified of it and hid it under a towel in my bedroom so that I wouldn't have to see it staring at me all the time. I did say thank you politely because Mummy gave her "say thank you" look. The second present was much better and it was easy to say thank you for that one. It was a small teddy bear but the special thing about it was it had a towelling coat that covered it completely so I could have it in the bath with me and it would still be dry to take to bed. "Can I have a bath now?" I asked and everyone laughed because it was only lunchtime. The third present was the best of all. It was a dressing gown which Daddy had found in India. It was white with a beautifully embroidered dragon down the back. I loved the dragon – it looked rather sad and I wondered if it was missing India – whatever India was. I asked Aunty Gwen – Mummy was much too busy talking to Daddy to be interrupted I had asked her but Mummy had said, "Not now, darling. I'm talking!" so I asked Aunty Gwen instead. We went together to look at the big globe of the world in Aunty Gwen's sitting room and found where India was. It looked quite small but then we found England and that looked even smaller. Aunty Gwen told me that it was very hot in India and the children were very poor – "They can have my cabbage!" I said – and they didn't need to wear many clothes. I wondered why they made dressing gowns but Aunty Gwen said that was enough questions so I knew it was time to keep quiet and not the right time to suggest Daddy should go back to India and leave them alone. I sensed that Mummy was pleased to have Daddy back even if I didn't like him much.

Kenneth's return to England brought about many more radical changes in my world – and Wendy's too. First, there was their future to consider. Kenneth was relieved to have the missing letter explained but the call to the mission field could not be ignored. Wendy quickly realised that her husband was determined to offer to go to Africa. He had heard of the need for missionaries to go to Ruanda – now Rwanda – and, given that the Sudan Mission was no more, he wanted to apply to the newly formed Ruanda Mission under the umbrella of the Church Missionary Society – CMS. Wendy never felt the Call in the way her husband did but she knew that where he went she must go too so sails were set for Africa. But there were stormy waters ahead. When Kenneth told Wendy's parents his plans for their future, his mother-in-law said, "We'll see about that!" His father-in-law was less vocal but no less distressed. Was there not plenty of missionary work to be done in England? Wendy was torn. Her mother refused to discuss the subject but when she realised that Kenneth was immovable her only comment was, "On your own heads be it!" I overheard the arguments and hoped Aunty Gwen was coming with us to Africa but I didn't dare ask.

Before we could set off for Africa's darkest interior Kenneth needed to finish his medical training. The war had come before he had done his year as a Registrar and there were two six-month placements to be completed. The first was in Edinburgh. "It's the other end of the world!" Wendy lamented. "Not as far as Africa," was her father's only comment.

We packed our bags and caught the train. We only took our clothes as we had been allocated a small furnished flat. I held my favourite teddy, called Monday because he came on the Monday before they set off for Edinburgh. There he was on the end of my bed. He never told me where he had come from and when I asked Aunty Gwen she said perhaps he just needed somebody to love him and he thought I would do. "You will be able to talk to him instead of Mr Knee-breeches when you go to Edinburgh," Aunty Gwen suggested. I thought this was a very good idea. The flat we were allocated was very small. I had a little bedroom off the sitting room. Every morning I had to go to Kindergarten. By this time Wendy was expecting David and was getting very tired. Kenneth and Wendy were very glad to have their own home however small and I was getting used to having Daddy there all the time. I had asked Mummy if she would ask Daddy to go back to the war so they could just be the two of them again but Mummy got quite cross and told me to pull myself together, Daddy was here to stay and they were very lucky he hadn't been killed. I told Monday all about it but he wisely kept quiet.

My parents were determined to make the most of their time together so when Kenneth was off duty, he and Wendy would go out in the evenings to various meetings. Jenny came to babysit. I liked Jenny and thought she was probably lonely all by herself in the sitting room so when the front door closed, I would hop out of bed and join her. We read stories and chatted and when it got really dark and time for my parents to come home, I hopped back into bed. One evening Mummy put on a nice dress, Jenny arrived and the front door closed with a click. I waited a minute and then climbed out of bed and went into the sitting room. I was just settling down with Jenny when the door opened and Daddy came back – he had forgotten his bible. He was cross. Smack! Smack! Very hard! On my bottom! "Don't let me catch you out of bed again!" Smack! "Jenny, she is not to get out of bed once she has been tucked up!" and the door shut – click. I cried. "It's not fair," I told Monday. "I was being kind to Jenny." But I had learnt my lesson and I didn't get out of bed again. I told Jesus I was sorry; I hadn't meant to be naughty and I asked him if He could please send Daddy away as Mummy never smacked me on my bottom, or anywhere else for that matter, and I didn't think it was a kind thing to do, but Daddy stayed and I was very careful to stick to the rules. I didn't like Kindergarten much. I didn't speak like all the other children so I tried not to speak at all but that felt lonely because there was nobody to play with so I changed my voice at school and talked like everyone else. I had a home voice and a school voice and that worked very well until Mabel came to play one day and Mummy heard my school voice. "Rachel, you are picking up an awful Scottish accent! What will your grandparents say?" But all was well because the six months were up and it was time to pack our bags and move, this time to Bristol for the next six months. I could leave my school voice in Edinburgh, I wouldn't need it in Bristol.

We moved into another small flat – there was hardly room for the four of us for David had been born. I wasn't sure how I felt about David. There was no room now to sit on Mummy's lap because David was always there. He cried a lot! But then I was allowed to have him on my lap and he stopped crying and held my finger very tightly and stared and stared at me and I found I loved him very much, and I still do! I loved him nearly as much as Monday, so when nobody was listening I whispered my secrets to him as well – until he began to talk and then it wasn't safe any more.

It was 1947 and one of the coldest winters on record. The flat was heated by a gas fire in the living room which was fed with coins in a metre. "This thing eats coins as fast as David uses up nappies!" Kenneth complained fishing in his pocket for yet another pound. Luckily for Wendy's sanity, Kenneth was working under a Consultant called Melville Capper married to May. One day he asked Kenneth how they were managing in the flat with the cold so Kenneth told him about the nappy situation – nappies everywhere, draped over a string hanging from one side of the room to the other, over chair backs, over the pram in the passageway and never seeming to get dry. There were no disposable nappies in those far-off days. Nappies were put to soak in a bucket, scrubbed by hand, wrung out and draped. Wendy was in despair and to make matters worse, if they could be worse, David had caught a cold and was whining and whining. Aunty May to the rescue. She and Uncle Melville had a big, warm house up the hill. All the damp nappies were bundled into a bag, David and I were bundled into warm clothes and Mummy walked us up the hill. What a relief! For a glorious two hours, we were warm and the nappies got dry, I was given different books to read and order was restored. Wendy walked the children, the pram, the bag of nappies and the books to be changed, up the hill three times a week until the weather improved and the six months in Bristol came to an end.

AFRICA

It was time to pack their bags for Africa so they moved back to the safety of Tomatin to Granny and Gaga – our affectionate name for our grandfather – and Aunty Gwen. But there were other goodbyes to be said. Kenneth's mother lived in Bristol with his sister Eileen. They must have visited them when they were living in Bristol. Grandma had white hair and spoke with an Irish accent. Aunty Eileen worked as a social worker in the hospital in Bristol. In those days she was called an Almoner. It was a very responsible job and I knew Aunty Eileen was important.

With Aunty Eileen at her home in Bristol

We went back to Bristol to say goodbye. I had just learnt how to do somersaults so I asked Aunty Eileen if she could do somersaults too. Aunty Eileen said she could but she couldn't show me because she was wearing a skirt and her knickers would show – she didn't seem to wear bloomers over her knickers like Aunty Gwen. I said I would shut one eye so I wouldn't see her knickers and keep one eye open to see the somersault – I had been practising shutting just one eye so I thought that would work well. Aunty Eileen didn't think it would work so I did my somersault on the carpet and Aunty Eileen clapped. We said goodbye. Little did we know that that would be the last time we saw either of them. Grandma died at the age of 83 and Aunty Eileen died of cancer of the kidneys. I remember the letter arriving in Africa telling us of Grandma's death but I don't remember any emotional reaction from either of my parents. Good missionaries just seemed to accept things, "God's will" and that was that (*I'm not sure how accurate I am with the details here*).

Saying goodbye to her parents and Gwen was a real ordeal for Wendy. She knew she had to go, Kenneth was her priority, but she had never envisaged her life as a missionary in Africa and what was she exposing her children to? Her mother was furious with Kenneth; her father was sadly resigned at the loss of his beloved youngest daughter who had always had a special place in his heart. Gwen was determined to visit. Irene Lockhart was to go with them. She was recovering from a broken love affair. She was a friend of the family, her father was their doctor. Many years later her niece, Elizabeth, was to marry my youngest brother, Michael, but that was many years in the future. It was decided that Wendy would then have a companion and Irene would recover in pastures new. Anyway, she could be usefully employed to teach me before I was packed off to boarding school. They all went down to the docks at Tilbury to see off the party on a Union Castle ship. It was all so exciting, seeing their cabins and standing on the deck waving, that I stopped crying and waved and waved as the boat sailed out and Aunty Gwen, Granny and Gaga got smaller and smaller. Mummy didn't stop crying for quite some time. Sometimes I would find her sitting quietly by herself, crying. I gave her lots of hugs and hoped that would help. Daddy didn't cry at all. I thought he should have tried to cry a little bit just to show solidarity but I don't think he had a clue what Mummy gave up for him.

The boat trip was a lot of fun and a holiday for all of us. There were games on board the ship and the sun came out and we all had to wear our hats and I got to wear my new sun dress. By this time David was running about and had to be tied to a chair on deck in case he fell overboard. Aunty Irene had a busy time chasing him about when he was untied. When they got to the Suez Canal little boats crowded the side of the ship and the gilli-gilli man came on board. He produced dozens of baby chicks out of his hat. Goodness knows what the passengers were supposed to do with the chicks but I was entranced. I begged to be allowed to keep the ball of yellow fluff I held in my hand but my mother was adamant, "No, Rachel, and this is a No that will not turn to Yes!" so I gave it back. Daddy had a cross look and told Mummy he did not want a scene. I wasn't sure what a scene was but I didn't want more smacks on my bottom so I kept very quiet even though I really did want a chick – company for Monday and something living to talk to! There was a man with a basket of snakes who played a tune on his pipe. When he played the snake stood up in the basket and waved about as though it was dancing. I watched from a good distance because I knew snakes could spit poison and I didn't want to be spat at. There were large straw sun hats, mats and baskets for sale, bracelets and necklaces, but the temptation was resisted and the ship sailed on down the canal.

And then one morning I woke up with a runny nose. I didn't feel very well and I had spots, lots of spots all over my tummy and arms and legs. I went into my parents' cabin. "Mummy, I've got spots!" Daddy sat bolt upright. "She's got German Measles!" he announced in his doctor's voice. I was put into a special cabin because I was In Quarantine for the rest of the voyage. A steward who had had German Measles brought my meals and stayed to chat if he wasn't too busy. I had crayons and colouring books but Aunty Irene hadn't had German Measles so she couldn't come and play - for which she was profoundly thankful, given what a good time she was having when David was safely tied up. Her broken heart had healed well! After four weeks on board, the ship sailed into Mombasa Port, the gangway was lowered and all the passengers disembarked.

Africa! Mummy and Daddy at our first stop in Kenya

I was collected from the cabin by a member of the crew and made to stand in a separate queue from the rest of the family. I was really scared that I was going to be sent away forever and never see them again. They waved at me from their queue. I cried but very quietly in case it caused "a scene". All was well. After passports had been checked the family were reunited and got on the train to go to our first Mission Station, Maseno, where we were to stay for three months covering for the missionaries who had gone on Leave to England. What an exciting journey that was. I shared a cabin with Aunty Irene and David. We had a bunk each and I sat on my bunk and stared out of the window hoping I would see an elephant. No elephants but giraffes away in the distance and lots of monkeys. Aunty Irene slept on the top bunk only she didn't sleep a wink – she was too terrified of falling off. She was beginning to think this whole idea of coming to Africa was not such a good one. She had not appreciated how stuck out in the bush she would find herself. She was only in her twenties and had hoped for an exciting social life. Perhaps nursing a broken heart in England would have been preferable. Too late!

With Aunty Irene and Mummy

It was a very different life and Wendy was not sure she really liked it either; she was thankful to have Irene to chat to. Of course, the flip side was it was nice to have people to work for her. The cook cooked in the kitchen which was an outhouse and had a wood-burning stove which belched out smoke as the door was always left open so the kitchen was a no-go area for Wendy. She gave the cook instructions every morning – somehow with much arm waving and shouting and nodding, Wendy could not speak Swahili and the cook's English was limited to say the least – miraculously meals appeared on the table. There was a nice African girl to look after David and Aunty Irene kept an eye on me with lessons in the morning and walks and games in the afternoon. I didn't know what my mother did all day but there was always tea in the garden and I ran races against Mummy. Well, we ran races until one day Wendy forgot to let me win and after that, I was not so keen on running races.

Three months later the doctor, who was to take over the hospital for the rest of the 12 months' leave, arrived and the Moynagh family packed up their bags and, with Aunty Irene in tow, off they went first to Kampala, where they stayed in the CMS missionary guest house. The lady who ran the Guest House was called Margaret. She was deaf so she couldn't hear the correct way to speak but she made a good stab at it. The words were all in a sort of jumble and I was very alarmed that I would be left with Margaret and I wouldn't be able to understand what I was saying. Mummy had told me it was rude to say "What" but I couldn't keep on saying "Pardon" so I just said "Yes" and "No" and hoped I had got the right one. They were not there for long and then they went on to a Mission Station called Shyra. They were to stay at Shyra for 15 months. The first three months we over-lapped with the Hindley family and the next year Kenneth took over the hospital while the Hindleys went on leave.

The Hindleys were big and noisy and there seemed to be an awful lot of them. They lived in a house on a hill and we lived in a house on the opposite hill with a road that led down to a roundabout planted with violets in between. The Hindley boys had bicycles and they tore down the hill, round the roundabout and back up the hill, shouting at each other, falling off their bikes and generally terrifying me. "Come and play," they invited but I was not going anywhere near them. There was another nice African girl to look after David and more lessons with Aunty Irene, walks in the afternoon, avoiding "Picadilly Circus", as the Hindleys called the roundabout, baths in a tin bath filled up with jugs of water and always a story before bed.

When it was Christmas, the Hindleys invited everybody on the mission station to Christmas lunch. There were two single ladies, one a nurse and the other a teacher working in the African school, our family and the Hindleys with their six children. By this time Wendy was pregnant and expecting Andrew; I was very excited at the thought of another baby. I hoped it would be a sister this time. When they got to the Hindleys' house on Christmas day there was the tallest tree I had ever seen – so tall that there was a special hole cut in the ceiling for the top of the tree. *(It was years later that I realised that the hole was always there and led to a storage loft area!)* I was not really surprised because everything about the Hindleys seemed big to me so the tree just confirmed my idea. The turkey on the table was huge and the pile of presents under the tree made my eyes nearly pop out of my head. After lunch, thirteen of them round the table – lucky they were missionaries so nobody minded it being thirteen – the wireless was turned on and they all stood to attention for the national anthem and then they had to listen to the King's speech, well the grown-ups listened and the Hindley children wriggled and whispered and got impatient and I tried to look as small as I could so that none of the children would notice me and hoped at least one of the presents might be for me. And one was a beautiful doll and a pram for her to sit in. I did not know that the pram had been recycled from the now grown-up Hindley girls. It had been cleaned up and repainted and, to a five-year-old, it looked new. I was speechless with delight. There would be room for Monday, my teddy, and Rosebud, my new doll, to ride in the pram together and when the new baby came she and my mother would be able to push the prams together. Goodness knows where Wendy was going to get a pram from, perhaps another Hindley cast-off!

So the days went past. The Hindleys packed their bags and left for England. But the Hindleys really deserve a paragraph to themselves – they were such a major part of my life. They were Big! And there were lots of them, Pat, Sue, Chris, Anthony, Peter and Tim.

Pat was always a distant figure almost grown-up and inhabiting the grown-ups' world. I loved Sue who was gentle and seemed almost lost in the family hurly-burly. Perhaps that explains her anorexia in her late teens. When her anorexia was in full swing and her weight was down to six stone – on a good week! - life at home must have been very stressful so her parents asked my parents if they would have her stay for a month or two hoping that she might eat at least something if she was out of the family's watchful eye. She was being threatened with hospital so being with the Moynaghs seemed a good idea. I must have been about 12 when Sue arrived and I became Sue's shadow. I had little idea why Sue had come to stay but I was determined to make the best of having a big sister. I remember one day when Sue and I were packed off for a walk and a picnic. In retrospect, it seems that Wendy was getting exasperated with trying to find family meals where

Sue would at least take one mouthful so a picnic would be good for her and get her out of Wendy's hair. The picnic was nice and there was a piece of Christmas cake to finish off with. "Sue ate every mouthful of cake!" I reported when we got home and I was quizzed as to what Sue had eaten!

One evening Daddy made himself a bedtime snack, a slice of bread and dripping. He left it on the dining room table while he locked up the house but when he got back it was gone. He couldn't find it anywhere. Eventually, he went into the back larder to see if he had left it there. No! Back to the dining room and there it was on the table. He rubbed his eyes; was he really that tired? Of course not – Sue had hidden it and then returned it! It became a family joke, "Anyone seen the bread and dripping?"

But back to the story I am telling you:

Christmas was over and the Hindleys had gone. Aunty Irene had done a good job teaching me. I could read quite well and write a bit and even do simple sums though I wasn't much good at the sums, never was, and never will be. There was a small school for missionary children over the Border in Uganda at Kabale. The school was run by four teachers ranging in age from twenty-five to thirty-five. The school took its name from "Winnie the Pooh" with two beautifully carved wooden rabbits standing back to back over the entrance and all the dormitories were named after characters from the book with Eeyore as the Sick Bay because he was always so miserable! There will be more about the school later on in this account. Sufficient to say Auntie Irene and I were packed off to school; Auntie Irene joined the staff and I joined the other thirty children. I did not like school and, at five years old, I felt I would rather stay at home but little girls of five do not have a choice and my trunk was packed and off we both went. The first term is a blank in my memories but I must have got through it somehow because the end of term came and all the children were lined up to walk down into the village to visit the Indian-run shop where we were to spend our pocket money. I bought a pencil and a rubber, a small dinky toy car for David and a bag of sweets. I seemed to finish my shopping before everyone else so I went outside and sat on the step next to an old African man who seemed to have a horrible cough. I offered him one of my sweets to help his cough and he seemed pleased. He ate the sweet but he still went on coughing. Trunks were packed and it was time for the holidays.

While I had been at school the Moynaghs had moved into the Hindleys' house at the top of the hill. David and I shared a bedroom off our parents' room with an adjoining door and another door into the corridor. It was a big room with plenty of space for my bed and David's cot. He was now 18 months old and into everything. Life settled into a routine with Kenneth busy in the hospital and learning the language both on the job and having lessons when he could fit them in. Wendy had regular language lessons and was taken under the wing of one of the few local women who could speak enough English to help Wendy find her feet visiting and attending Women's Meetings. Every Sunday we went to Church. There were no pews, only a few hard benches, so we took our folding chairs with them. Services went on for a long time, up to three hours, so I was allowed to go out with Theresa, who looked after David, before the sermon. Even so, I was not very enthusiastic about Church – the Africans always wanted to touch my hair – it was so different from theirs! There was no organ so somebody banged a drum to keep everyone in time. One Sunday morning I said I didn't want to go to Church as I didn't feel very well. I heard my parents talking about it - "Do you think she is just trying to wriggle out of going?" "No, I don't think so. She is looking rather pale." "Well, why don't we let her stay at home for once? She will be fine – the house staff will be around and she can sit quietly and read her book. Give her a couple of aspirin. That should do the trick!" So they left me on the window seat looking out over the hills. If I shut my eyes even all these years later I can still see that view. At the time I didn't realise what was meant by a view but at five years old I just knew I had a headache and all I wanted to do was sit by the window and look out at the blue mountains in the distance. I watched the weaver birds with their yellow heads building their nests and was lulled by the cooing pigeons until I fell asleep. When my parents got back from Church they found me curled up where they had left me so they popped me into bed with another aspirin feeling sure I would be better in the morning. Little did any of them know what a change in their lives the morning would bring.

I had my bed opposite the door to my parents' room. Early in the morning, I woke up. The sun was shining through the window and I heard the girl who worked in the house knock on my parents' other door, draw back their curtains and put the early morning tray of tea on the bedside table. Time to get up. I sat up – but I couldn't sit up. Nothing would work (*I do not remember the next few months until we got to Uganda then my memories come back as sharp as yesterday's*). Somehow I fell out of bed onto the floor. I was stuck. I really was stuck. I couldn't make anything work – not my arms or my legs. I didn't know what to do so I did the only thing possible – I called for help. My mother came into the room in her nightie, "Goodness!" she said, "What on earth are you doing on the floor? Jump up quick while I sort out David!" "I can't!" I wailed. Poor Mummy froze. And that is when the world shifted and was never the same again.

During his medical training, Kenneth had been to a lecture by an orthopaedic surgeon called Professor Seddon.

He had a particular interest in what was then called Infantile Paralysis and he explained that, when paralysis set in, it was very important to keep the affected muscles moving so that they did not become permanently paralysed. Remembering this, three times a day Kenneth carried me into the bathroom, put me into a warm bath and moved my limbs. I'm told I screamed from the moment he walked into the room until the moment he walked out. We can only imagine how he must have felt. Wendy was five months pregnant with Andrew at the time. There was consternation throughout the mission field as the news spread. Anxious parents watched over their own children. It was decided that I had picked up polio from the old African man on the steps. What a price to pay for sharing a bag of sweets! How many other children were going to share the same fate? Parents waited and watched. No other children caught it and the children all went back to school. I was beginning to get back some movement. I had learnt to use my right hand, which worked, to uncurl my fingers on my left hand – the first of a lifetime of finding coping strategies - and one wonderful day, when Mummy bent over to kiss me goodnight, I managed to get my right arm round my mother's neck, pick up my left hand and pull it up enough to give my mum a hug. A hug! The first hug in two months! But progress needs a plan. Bags were packed and Wendy, David and I and Theresa to look after David, all set off for Kampala where I was to spend a month in hospital.

The hospital bed was out on the veranda during the day and pushed inside for the night. There was a lot to look at during the day and I loved watching the hummingbirds with their long beaks flitting about amongst the bougainvillaea flowers. The trumpet-shaped flowers of the Deadly Nightshade grew in profusion on the bush just beyond the balcony rail and there were weaver birds and brightly coloured starlings busy about their daily chores full of conversations with the constant background cooing of the doves, forever the sound that brings back Africa. The nurses were in and out, too busy to be much company but Wendy, by this time heavily pregnant, spent a lot of time sitting peacefully by my bed.

She must have been wondering what sort of future lay before this beautiful, paralysed child of hers. One thing was certain – she would not become a spoilt child! So there were daily battles over Egg Custard. I hated Egg Custard – slimy and wobbly and yellow! But it was on the menu and I was not going to grow up to be fussy so I had to eat it. I ate it and was sick. The mess was cleared up and another bowl was brought. I ate it and was not sick but I hated it all the same. A Nice Elderly Missionary was going On Leave and was to fly to England so it was decided that I would make the three-day flight with her. Wendy was far too pregnant to fly too and anyway, there were Kenneth and David and Missionary Work to consider. Arrangements were made with the Airline – BOAC. In those days there were ordinary planes and then there were Flying Boats. These huge planes took off from the designated area at Entebbe. A suitcase was packed, though there was precious little a bed-ridden five-year-old had to pack. Clutching Monday, I was shipped off to Auntie Gwen in England. Hard to imagine how Wendy must have felt as she said goodbye to her firstborn. The plane took off with great plumes of water masking any view from the windows but I waved all the same. The Nice Elderly Missionary, Monday and I settled back in our seats for the next three days.

It was raining when the plane splashed down at Southampton docks. My grandparents and Aunty Gwen were there to meet me. When the news of my polio had reached her grandmother she had written back to her daughter reminding her that she had been told that nothing good would come of this ridiculous call to be a missionary. Experience had proved that Africa was a dangerous place – remember that Wendy's father had contracted Blackwater Fever when he had visited Gwen in Africa. Wendy had only herself to blame that I had caught Polio. But what was done was done and Grandmother put on her fur coat, found her gloves and her umbrella and set off to meet the precious little girl she had waved goodbye to so reluctantly eighteen months previously. There was an ambulance to collect me. The grandparents and Aunty Gwen thanked the Nice Elderly Missionary for looking after me and followed the ambulance all the way to The Wingfield Morris Hospital in Oxford. The ambulance drew into the parking bays and Grandfather parked his car next to it. It was dark but they made their way to the entrance – well Aunty Gwen and Grandmother made their way. Grandfather did not see the hole in the road left by the workmen the previous day. When Grandmother and Aunty Gwen turned round to see where Grandfather was he had vanished. He was down the hole! The ambulance men deposited me inside the door and went back to pull Grandfather out of the hole, find another stretcher and take him off to A&E. Grandmother left Aunty Gwen with me and went off to find Grandfather who was surprised to find himself behind a curtain on a stretcher. He had been knocked out cold.

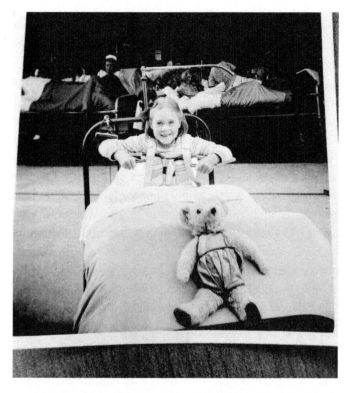

Back in England, 9 months after being diagnosed
with Polio in the hospital in Oxford

And so began the nine months I lived in the hospital. Every weekend Aunty Gwen drove from Bromley, South London, to Oxford to visit. Once a month the Grandparents visited as well. Very slowly I began to get more movement in my arms and legs. There were lessons in the morning. Claire lived in the next bed. She was ten so quite old really but I was good at reading so we read to each other and helped each other with the difficult sums – well Claire did the sums and then told me what the answers were and the teacher was pleased with my progress. Three times a week children from the ward were taken to the swimming pool in the Physio department and put through their exercises underwater. The other two days they had to go to the Physio room and do exercises there. I much preferred the pool. My arms and legs didn't feel so heavy in the water and it was easier to make them work than it was on land. Each weekend Aunty Gwen would make me learn a verse from the Bible. There wasn't much Christian teaching going on in the ward and Aunty Gwen wanted to make sure I was steered along the right path. She started with Psalm 23 and progressed to more demanding passages. I was anxious to please so I learnt my verses and on Fridays, Claire had to test me so that Aunty Gwen would be pleased when she came the next day.

Life slipped into a comfortable routine and I forgot about Africa and my parents and David. When you are five years old all that matters is the immediate present. Even the news of Andrew's arrival didn't cause much of an impact. Every month my physiotherapist wrote a letter to Africa reporting on my progress. It is hard to imagine what went through Wendy's mind as she read the monthly reports and the letters from her sister telling her about her daughter. How she must have longed for those letters. How she must have looked for progress. Or did she feel as dislocated from her daughter as I did from her?

And there was progress. As the months went by I learnt to sit up, hold a pencil and write my own letters - very short and written under considerable duress! When the summer came the beds were pushed outside under the big tree. The ward had big, floor-to-ceiling, glass doors which were opened right up so that the beds could be pushed outside quite easily.

In the garden where we would be wheeled out in our beds

One day, when they were all under the tree, I saw a man coming across the grass holding a contraption. He marched straight up to my bed. "Here we are, young lady," he said. He and the nurse buckled me into what was called an arm splint. Actually, it was more of a brace. Bars went down the front and the back and straps went round my back and buckled up down my front – there must have been four straps. There were two armrests that stuck out from either side and kept my arms up at shoulder height. I was meant to keep my arms on the rests all the time but of course, I didn't. When nobody was looking I took them off but the problem was I wasn't strong enough to lift them back on again so there I would be, trussed up like a chicken with my arms sort of dangling. It was all most uncomfortable and I quickly learned how to manage with my arms on the rests. Then the time came for a splint to be fitted on my right leg to keep my foot from dropping – my left leg was managing quite nicely and was getting quite strong by now what with all the exercises. The splint was made up of a small bar that slotted into a hole in the shoe; there were bars up the side of my leg which attached to a circle of leather just below my knee; a spring was fitted from the toe of the shoe to the leather circle below my knee to hold up my foot. My left leg was strong enough to manage on its own. I had to walk between parallel bars in the special physio room. There was a mirror in front of the bars so that I could see what I looked like walking. What a funny little girl I looked struggling along between the bars. How I managed the walking with my arms up on the splints defies imagination. The arm splints must have come off when it was walking time. I wore the splint on my leg until I was sixteen. How I longed for shoes that were not lace-ups! No wonder my cupboards are always full of shoes!

So the summer came and all the talk in the ward was about the summer ball. I listened as the nurses made my bed. "What are you going to wear?" "Are you going with Peter or Paul?" Hair was to be specially done and nails were to be painted and it was all very exciting. I asked if there would be balloons and a special cake but it wasn't that sort of party which I thought was rather disappointing for the nurses. The evening came and, in all the excitement, the nurses forgot to draw the curtains across the big windows looking out over the lawn and the tree where the beds were put on sunny days. I lay in my bed and watched the nurses walking past with the doctors. They wore beautiful long dresses of all different colours and they didn't look at all as they looked in their uniforms. Some of them were holding hands and there was lots of smiling and even some kissing! As the light was fading one couple sauntered by the window and onto the grass under the tree. Then they lay down under the tree. I thought they must be tired but then they started rolling about and then the doctor started rolling about on top of the nurse and I began to get really worried he might squash her flat so I thought I ought to do something about it. I called the night nurse who was on duty and showed her what was going on. "Oh, help!" said the nurse. "Who forgot to draw the curtains?" and with a swish, the curtains were pulled across the window. "What about the squashed nurse?" I asked but the nurse on duty had gone back to being on duty somewhere else so I thought it was time to go to sleep.

Nine months went by and then the great day came when it was time to go home to Tomatin and live with my grandparents and Aunty Gwen.

Back with Granny in Tomatin after a year in hospital

I was very excited and a little bit worried too. Would Aunty Gwen know how to put on my arm splints and my leg splint? Would I manage to walk quickly enough not to get left behind if they went shopping? How would I climb up the stairs to go to bed? But Aunty Gwen had thought about all those things. She was shown how to put on the splints by the nurse; there was a wheelchair for going out; Grandpa would carry me up the stairs for bed and I would learn how to climb down the stairs slowly, slowly. So they went back to Tomatin and I settled down there for the next year. I have to confess it was a very happy year. I was the centre of attention and never gave a thought to the family in faraway Africa. But despite an overall feeling of happiness, there are only snap-shot memories of that year. There was a trip to the Isle of Wight. We stayed in a small hotel and one morning Aunty Gwen and I both woke up too early to have breakfast so Aunty Gwen popped me into the wheelchair and we went to the beach. I watched Aunty Gwen have a before-breakfast swim. Aunty Gwen said it was freezing cold but "bracing" - not that I had any idea what "bracing" meant! We hurried back to the hotel and found Granny and Grandpa just coming down to the dining room and they were very surprised to find we had already been down to the beach and it all felt like a big adventure!

With Aunty Gwen on the Isle of Wight

Aunty Gwen used to go riding once a week. A man brought a horse to the front gate and Aunty Gwen looked wonderfully smart in her riding outfit. She even had a whip! Twice a week a car picked me up and took me to the hospital for exercise. There were two physiotherapists there who would take me through my paces. One of them was not very nice – she always started off the sessions by pulling each of my fingers until it cracked. There didn't seem much point in this and it hurt and I dreaded the days when she was on duty. To this day I hate the sound of clicking fingers. But I made slow but steady progress. I learnt to crawl up the stairs and come down again very slowly. Aunty Gwen taught me to play a tune on the piano which was good to get my fingers moving. I helped my grandfather pick gooseberries and blackcurrants from the garden and I searched for eggs in the straw in the hen house. Sometimes Uncle Martin would come for tea in the garden and he would always bring shrimps which we would eat with brown bread and butter. We spent Christmas with Aunty Doris and Uncle Oliver and Nanny and Molly. Molly cooked a big turkey and all the rest of the Christmas food and Nanny kept an eye on Mervyn, Brian and Denham, my three cousins. I felt safest in the Kitchen where I helped Molly do all the hard work while the grown-ups chatted in the posh Drawing-room. It was all very safe and English and middle class with help in the house, predictable seasons and a return to the way of life I had enjoyed for the first four years of my life. Africa became little more than a memory. Of course, I must have missed my parents. My mother wrote to me every week and told me about David and about how Andrew was beginning to walk but it all seemed more like a story than real life. Only when I was writing this did David tell me how ill Andrew had been as a baby and that Mummy had thought she was going to lose him but that some of the local Christians had come in and prayed for him and he had pulled through and made a good recovery though he always suffered from asthma and dreadful eczema;

I can remember the bandages on his arms and legs to stop him from scratching, poor little boy.

I was surrounded with love and had easily adapted to life without the African family who was so remote they were more like a story.

But I needed to get back to the family and so the date was set for my return. A suitable returning missionary must have been found to escort me back again, my case was packed and there were tears as I was bundled onto the plane clutching Monday and wondering how I would manage without Aunty Gwen. There had been a final visit to Oxford to see Professor Seddon who decided that my right arm was strong enough to do without the arm splint and a new one was made with only one wing for my left arm, but the leg splint was left in place. I had to wear shoes that had thick enough heels for the splint to fit into and Aunty Gwen packed several pairs of increasing sizes so that there would be shoes for me to grow into. How I hated those clumping shoes. How I longed for sandals like all the other children. There had been regular letters from Gwen to her sister and Wendy was prepared for the splints but can letters really prepare you? She hadn't seen her daughter for eighteen months. So much had changed. Had she really taken into account my limitations, my clumsy gait, the intrusive splints? One thing was certain – I would be treated like every other child. I would do everything I could, I would not be spoilt in any way and there would be no concessions either at home or at school. There were hugs at the Airport in Kampala. David had grown and seemed really pleased to see me but more pleased with the dinky car I gave him. Andrew was only eighteen months old so he didn't take much notice of me. Mummy cried. I overheard her say, "Oh, Kenneth, we'll have to do something about her weight!" I was really worried too. Would Mummy know how to put on my arm splint with all its straps and buckles? Most of all would they really want me back? There wasn't even a wheelchair. "You won't need one now. It is important that you walk everywhere," said Daddy firmly. We got in the car and drove back, all the way to Kigeme which was to be our home for the next three years – the Hindleys were back from their time in England and back in their house in Shyra.

It was difficult to settle back into the family. My parents were busy missionaries and we were looked after by a very nice African woman called Dora - Theresa didn't want to go and live in Kigeme so she went back to Shyra and Dora took her place. During the years at Kigeme, there were various highlights. I had to learn to ride a bike. I wasn't particularly keen on this idea but it seemed to be a rite of passage. A lad called Joseph, who helped in the garden, was delegated the task of helping me. Goodness knows where the bike came from but the saddle was adjusted and I climbed on. I remember being terrified. Joseph held on tight. "Pedal!" came the command. I pedalled – round and round the circular drive we went, me pedalling, Joseph balancing me. Joseph was endlessly patient. There was no chance of giving up – I was to pedal until Joseph could let go. And eventually, I got the hang of it and joined my brothers on bike rides and games that involved bikes.

Back in Africa

Joseph went back to gardening, a far more leisurely pursuit. One day two Golden Crested Crane chicks were delivered to the back door. Why Wendy agreed to keep them remains a mystery but she did so a run had to be made for them. Joseph was called in to help. They grew into the most beautiful birds with sharp beaks and vicious intentions. I kept my distance. After the children had been pecked, comforted, and cleaned up with plenty of Dettol, Wendy decided they would be better off, and the family would be safer, if they were released from their cage so the run was dismantled and the birds were free to go. However, life in the garden was too comfortable to be sacrificed so they continued to terrorise the family for several months. They were there and then they weren't there and no explanation as to their whereabouts was given! The other pet delivered to the back door was a baby monkey. Memories of it are vague; its thieving, destructive nature soon outweighed its cuteness and it too was given short shrift.

There were other games: I thought that now I could ride my bike we could be a circus. David could do tricks on his bike and, at six years old, he was most cooperative – until I told him he had to ride standing up and not holding on. He stood up, let go and fell off. Never mind! How about Andrew, aged just four, taking his part? He could do the splits. I held one leg, and David held the other! We pulled. Andrew thought he was going to come apart in the middle so he screamed. Both parents were convinced something awful had happened and arrived on the scene to see what was going on. They were cross and told me I was old enough to know better. I spent quite a long time in my bedroom and decided that was not one of my better suggestions.

Kenneth needed an outlet for his artistic abilities be it painting, building or storytelling. He won his battle over the breeze blocks in the new nurses' wing. He told wonderful stories in the car on the long car journeys to and from school and many of the missionary children still remember being entertained. Every Christmas, on Christmas Eve, when we children were in bed and Father Christmas was busy filling up stockings, he created a picture to hang up above the fireplace. Sometimes he used pastels, sometimes silhouettes cut out of black paper and stuck onto a blue sheet, always different, always moving and always special. It was such an important part of Christmas.

He passed this innovative streak on to his youngest son who was a little boy full of curiosity. One day Michael was bored, left out of the games his older siblings were playing and wise enough to keep right out of anything that suggested a circus. He asked his father what to do. The response was typical, "Find a long stick, look for a hole in the garden and poke the stick down the hole. You never know, you might find a toad!" A brilliant idea. Michael went off to find a stick and a hole and his father settled down in his study. Peace reigned. Not for long. Michael catapulted into the room, hands full, "Daddy, Daddy two toads! Look!" Who was most surprised, father or son?

There were old, empty oil drums placed in strategic spots around the house to catch the rainwater. It had been a very wet season and the drums were pleasingly full. Michael used his trusted toad stick as a fishing rod. He found some string – the loo was a long drop outside, the "door" facing away from the house and shielded by a hedge, a string was attached to a post placed at the entrance to the little house on the opposite side from the "door". To show people that the loo was occupied the string was pulled across the path and attached to a post on the other side of the entrance; it was primitive but effective as long as people remembered to hang up and un-hang the string, and as long as the important piece of string was left in place. But Michael needed a piece of string for his fishing rod and this seemed ideal to him. So, he detached the string, found a pin in the pot on his mother's desk, bent it a bit and tied it on to the string. It took a long time to make the fishing rod but eventually he was ready to go fishing. He found a nice full oil drum and lent over the rim to see if he could see any stray fish that had lost their way and ended up in the water. He lost his balance. Head in the water, feet waving frantically. What a blessing the gardener was sauntering past. He saw the legs waving, heard the bubbles, pulled him out by his feet, wiped his face with the cloth used to clean the lawnmower and sent him indoors with strict orders not to go fishing again. The story only came to light when I needed to go to the loo and there was no string. The fishing rod and its creator were found by the oil drum. I scooped up my little brother, restored the string to its rightful place and promised not to tell their parents provided Michael did not go fishing again. The gardener was not so discreet but Wendy was so relieved that her son had not drowned that no more was said.

But at the beginning of their time at Kigeme, I was eight years old and could not be kept at home, so when the new term started, off I went back to school in Kabale where the Aunties were ready to welcome me. I was not really surprised to be sent away so soon. I realised that I was different in that I needed extra attention – my arm splint for one thing, my shoes and leg splint for another. I had tried very hard to be good but obviously not good enough – this was years before I set up the circus. I talked to Monday about the whole situation but, though he was a very good listener, he didn't come up with any advice so my trunk was packed and we set off on the two-day journey to Kabale, on the border of Uganda and Rwanda. The journey was accomplished with one night on the way to pick up Christopher and Anthony Hindley. I had to say goodbye to my mother at home as she could not leave the two little boys – it seemed to me she could never leave them. I cried a lot but very quietly so as not to be a nuisance. Monday got very wet and would have protested if he had been able. I was too frightened of the Hindley boys to cry when they arrived at the school and I had to say goodbye to my father too. At eight years old I understood that three months away from home was a long time.

SCHOOL DAYS

Kabale Prep School was a very happy place. As I have told you the school itself was named after the characters in "The House at Pooh Corner" with two beautifully carved rabbits standing back to back above the entrance porch. Each dormitory was named after one of the characters so I started in Piglet and then moved up to Rabbit. We were there for three months at a time with no half-term breaks and very rare visits from parents – visits were unsettling and made children cry so they weren't encouraged. The four teachers were young and dedicated to their work – this was their call to the mission field and was just as important as converting the heathen; probably a lot more fun than learning a different language and living on an isolated mission station in the back of beyond. Certainly, Aunty Irene, who was not needed to teach me and so moved on to the staff of the school, thought it was a lot more fun than being stuck out in the blue with Wendy and one small child to teach. Her broken heart had quite recovered and she eventually married a tea planter. The school was on the route from Kampala, the capital of Uganda, to Rwanda and Burundi so there were often visitors passing through. More about the visitors later. Along with the dormitories, there was a large dining room with long tables and benches to sit on, difficult for me as I found it hard to get my leg in its calliper over the bench, but I managed because I wasn't going to be different. There was just one set of stairs which lead up into the Prayer Room. This was a very special room and you were only allowed up if you were with one of the Aunties.

All the children at Kabale Prep School - Me, middle row, 3rd from left

In the Prayer Room, you had to tell God all about the naughty things you had done. You had to tell the Aunties and the other children too. I didn't think this was a very good idea. I didn't mind telling Jesus, though it seemed a bit of a waste of time given that He knew anyway, but I didn't think it was anyone else's business. Above everything, I was a child who wanted to fit in but I didn't have sins I wanted to share. I didn't want everyone to know that sometimes I pretended to have a headache so that I could go to the sick room and have toast for breakfast; or that I didn't like Angela so I borrowed her best pencil and broke the point on purpose; or that I didn't want John to sit next to me so I told a lie and said I was keeping the seat for David. These were private sins. But I was resourceful. I said I had been very cross when I had only been a little bit cross and that seemed to satisfy everybody. I got good at making up sins and then repenting of them and this ensured I fitted in. But I did like going up into the Prayer Room – it was peaceful up there and I could look out of the window and see everyone moving about below me, little people doing little things.

Not only was there the main building, but there were also two other buildings – the classroom block which was close to the main house, and the Senior dormitories which, for me, seemed quite a long way away. When I went back to school after polio, I had to move into the Senior Dormitory despite the walk across the lawn, under the huge avocado pear tree, all in the early morning mist, a safari for a little girl in a calliper. I was always last to get to breakfast but they always waited for me before they said grace so that was all right. It was very important to keep an eye on children's insides and make sure they were working properly so after breakfast everyone lined up in front of Auntie Muriel, the school nurse. Her question was, "Have you been?" If the answer was yes, then off we scampered to lessons. If the answer was no, then we waited in another queue for a spoonful of horrible milk of magnesia which was guaranteed a yes the next day. Some lucky thin children had spoonfuls of cod liver oil and malt, but I certainly wasn't one of those.

The days slipped by in a comfortable routine. In the mornings there were lessons. Auntie Barbara took the younger children and Auntie Joy was responsible for the older ones. After lunch, there was a rest under the big pepper tree. Everyone collected a mat and found a place to unroll it. Rest was forty minutes long. For the first twenty minutes, they all had to lie still and have a snooze. I liked that; I didn't snooze but I did make up stories in my head which I planned to tell Michael when I got home. By the time I did get home of course I had forgotten them and anyway Michael wasn't the least bit interested.

For the second half of rest time, we were allowed one toy to play with and everyone could choose one sweet. I could never decide whether to suck the sweet while I was making up stories or when I was reading my book. So many difficult decisions when you are eight. The Auntie on duty sat in a deck chair and read her book or did her knitting or wrote letters home to England. After rest it was time for organised games which I did my best to join in with and then there was bread and tree-tomato jam for tea. The Aunties had their tea on a table with a cloth on it under a different pepper tree and they had cucumber sandwiches. *(I know that because, for six months, I was an Auntie between leaving school and going to Cambridge)*

One day Auntie Joy called me into her special room and told me that my parents were going to pick me up the very next day. For one wonderful moment, I thought they must have got lonely without me and were taking me home. Wishful thinking. The doctor who had looked after me in Oxford was at a conference in Kampala and had agreed to see me to assess how I was getting on. The adults called it "an answer to prayer". I just thought it was an unexpected bit of good luck. Professor Seddon examined me and told my parents he did not think I would ever have much more strength in my left arm and it was time to take off the arm splint and let me find ways to compensate. I still find that I can do most things if I tighten my tummy muscles enough – well until I had a stroke which hasn't helped at all.

What a happy day! We went to the posh hotel for tea to celebrate and then got in the car and drove the five hours back to school. No arm splint! I looked nearly the same as everyone else.

There were special highlights that broke up the terms. Although the children did not go home for half-term there were half-term treats. Two of these were particularly memorable.

A picnic was arranged and we were to walk to Crystal Hill where we could find pieces of crystal to bring home with us. It was a long walk for all of them, a good hour and a half, so for me, it was a nightmare. But the rule was that I was to do what everyone else did so I tied my jersey around my waist and set off with everyone else. One of the Aunties stayed at the back with me, I was inevitably always last, but it was almost worth the walk. The sun on the hillside picked up the crystal and the whole hill glinted and sparkled. I thought it was a magic hill, a place where surely the fairies must live – and surely there must be fairies in Africa. Aunty Gwen said there were and Auntie Gwen knew things like that. They probably spoke a different language but they were sure to live on Crystal Hill. Everyone set about collecting pieces of crystal. The story goes that in Idi Amin's time, when there was the purge of the Indian tradesmen and many of them left Uganda and came to England, one enterprising Indian passed off his diamonds by hiding them in his son's tin of collected "treasures"! Crystals and diamonds were hard to tell apart. Certainly, we all vied with each other to see who could find the biggest, shiniest, most beautifully coloured piece. We all had paper bags into which we put our collections. I looked carefully behind the big rocks to see if any fairies were hiding but I couldn't see any. I wasn't surprised as I knew fairies were very shy and hid away – I knew exactly how they felt! After the picnic lunch, it was rest time and everyone sat quietly and sorted through their treasures keeping only the best pieces to carry back to school. And then it was the long trek back again; I was, exhausted and last as usual.

The second half-term adventure was a trip to Sharps Island. Dr and Mrs Sharp were two of the first missionaries to go to Kabale as part of the Ruanda Mission Out Reach. Their special interest was in Leprosy and they set up a leper colony on one of the Islands in the Lake. The Sharps lived on a nearby island and Mrs Sharp had turned the island into a wonderful garden. It became a sanctuary for tired missionaries. There was a guest room away from the main house and the Aunties, among other missionaries, used it as a retreat when they had a weekend off from school.

Once a year the children from the school were invited to spend a day on the island. After breakfast and the "have you been" queue, we were hustled and bustled into jerseys and shoes and each of us was given our bathers wrapped in a towel. Each of us put the rolled-up towel in the communal basket and climbed up into the school lorry which took us down to the lake. There were three canoes waiting to take us across to the island. The canoes were hollowed-out tree trunks and we sat on low wooden seats down each side of the canoe. Each canoe had one Auntie in charge and the fourth lucky Auntie went in Dr Sharp's accompanying motorboat. I tried very hard not to cry when I realised I was going to have to climb into the canoe. It wobbled horribly and I wasn't very good at swimming. This was most definitely an emergency and I knew what to do in an emergency – pray! The African man who was paddling the canoe saw the tears of a little girl with a calliper on her leg. He moved everyone out of the way, sidled along the canoe and held out his arms to me. He lifted me into the boat, smiled at me and went back to his place at the back of the canoe. Sometimes God does answer the prayers of little girls. The canoe wobbled; I held on tight to the edge; the big boys lent over the side to see if they could see a crocodile; the canoe wobbled even more and the Aunties in charge got cross. There weren't any crocodiles and the journey was safely accomplished. The kind man deposited me safely on the island without anybody noticing – they were all too busy finding their towels in the basket.

First, there were glasses of orange to drink outside the main house. A table had been set up under one of the trees. The lawn sloped down to the path at the water's edge bordered by flower beds full of the brightness of canna lilies, roses, Michaelmas daisies, dahlias – a riot of colour, everything growing in profusion with no regard for the seasons. There were secret places to explore in the morning and then lunch – packets of sandwiches handed to each of us – under the tree near the house.

In the afternoon everyone went swimming. I wasn't very keen on swimming. The mud squelched between my toes and I was scared of the leeches that attached themselves to my legs and got fatter and fatter with the blood they were sucking. But all was well – no leeches and I made sure I stayed close to the bank. When it was time to get out one of the Aunties blew a whistle – boys behind one bush, girls behind another, into our clothes and then up to the house for tea. There were different sorts of cake to choose from and more sandwiches this time for the grown-ups. Then it was time to go back to school. Into the canoes again and I was terrified all over again but strong arms lifted me into the boat and the big boys were too tired to look for crocodiles so the return journey was much less wobbly. Everyone had eaten so much all day that nobody wanted much supper and everyone was glad to tumble into bed. I said a private thank you to God for not letting me fall overboard and drown and then I went to sleep and dreamt of strong arms and crocodiles.

Missionaries are human and missionary men need wives. Where better to look than at the four single girls who taught in a missionary school? So the young men came a-courting. I was a nosy little girl who watched people without their knowing they were being watched. When visitors came to KPS I was always interested. The Aunties were young and pretty and very Christian so it wasn't surprising that the unmarried male missionaries found lots of valid reasons to visit. First came Reg. After two or three visits, he and Auntie Joy went down to the bottom of the garden. I saw them bow their heads and put their hands together so I knew they were praying. Then they came back up the garden and told the other Aunties they were going to get married. I was lurking near the table under the pepper tree so I heard what they were saying. The other Aunties were delighted. Some months later Auntie Joy asked me to be her bridesmaid. I wore a long, pale green dress which hid my calliper and I felt beautiful and important.

So that was Uncle Reg and Auntie Joy. Next, Kenneth came a-calling. He and Auntie Barbara went up into the Prayer Room so they must have prayed. They came down and told the Aunties that they were going to get married. I just happened to be outside the Staff Room so I heard all the Aunties being very pleased. Bert was the next visitor. Auntie Heather didn't seem to want to pray. She went into the bathroom and I looked through the semi-open door and saw her washing Uncle Bert's back. Then they came out and said they were going to get married. It all seemed a very satisfactory way to agree to get married and live happily ever after. I thought I would like to find a nice man and pray – and wash his back – and get married.

Like every school there were lessons and there was playtime. When I started school before I had polio, I was only six so I was one of the younger ones. There was a gang of big boys made up of Chris, Michael, David and Stephen. They had a secret hide-out made from a hollowed-out space under a large bush. When they were well out of the way I peered into the bush and saw the magical space where they had put an old piece of sacking as a carpet and taken some mugs from the dining room. When I got older and was one of the big ones, I used the secret hideaway. I found old bits of china and played imaginative games and felt safe from the rest of the world. But when I was six I stood in awe of the big boys. Chris used to tease me so I was scared of him but Stephen was always kind and smiled at me and when he smiled I felt really happy. I wondered if he would like to pray with me and then we could get married when we were older but he never asked and then he left the school and I didn't see him again. (*Nearly sixty years later I met him again at a school reunion and told him how I had hero-worshipped him when I was six. He smiled and said, "Well I had quite a thing for you because you always smiled at me!" That was a really nice full-stop.*)

The children were at school for three months at a stretch so birthdays were celebrated away from home. Early in the morning, the two best friends of the birthday boy/girl got up and went out into the garden with one of the Aunties to pick flowers to decorate the throne that would be put at the head of the table for breakfast. Armed with armfuls of greenery they set about winding it all over the chair. Presents were put on the table. The birthday person chose two people to sit next to them. I always hoped I would be chosen but I wasn't anybody's best friend, just everybody's friend, so I watched from further down the table. Everyone sang "Happy Birthday" as loudly as they could. At tea time there was always a special cake. The birthday person was allowed to choose whatever shape they wanted and there were some spectacular creations. The boys chose cars mostly and the girls liked dolls' houses. I would have chosen Crystal Hill or the canoe for Sharps' Island but my birthday was just before Christmas, holiday time, and Mummy stuck to a round cake – creations were way beyond her!

My calliper had been adapted after my visit to Kampala under the instruction of Professor Seddon so that it was not so obtrusive and I felt a little more normal. I was to remain like that until I was 16 – in those growing years I was careful not to look in the mirror at my reflection from the waist down.

Photos that showed the calliper were ignored where possible.

The years at KPS were happy ones. I learnt to keep up with everyone else and no concessions were made for my limitations. My walking improved with time and, though my weight was always to be a problem, it was kept more or less under control. I found all sorts of coping strategies which stood me in good stead for the following years. Most especially I developed my own personal relationship with God, perhaps less conventional than my parents would have liked but real nonetheless. I became mostly independent and did not ask for help more than was absolutely necessary.

HOME LEAVE
AND HOLIDAYS

So the years at school slipped past and when I was 10 it was time for Home Leave and the family packed their bags and set off for England. Granny had written to Wendy apologising for her attitude and was determined to make her months with the family happy ones. Michael was 18 months old and still in nappies so one of the last pieces of luggage to go in the car was his nappy bag. When the family got to Kampala, where they were to board the plane to England, there were the inevitable last bits of shopping to do so they went into Kampala and parked the car. Somehow somebody broke into the car and stole the bag of nappies – and Monday! How disappointing to go to all that trouble and end up with a bag of nappies and one teddy bear. Yes, Monday had been packed in the bag and now he was gone. Despite being 10 and "too big for teddy bears", Monday was my confident and I was inconsolable. How could I go to England without Monday? He had been everywhere with me – hospital; to stay with me at Tomatin, my grandparents' home; to KPS. He had accompanied me through all my adventures and now he had gone. "Tears won't bring him back," Mummy said. I pulled myself together but I never got over the loss of Monday.

So back to Tomatin the family went. The journey back to England took three days with night stops in Benghazi and Malta. In Malta, we stayed in a high-rise hotel. David climbed out of the window eight floors up and sat on the sill with his legs dangling. When Wendy turned around and saw him, her shout of horror nearly had disastrous results – it gave poor David such a fright that if his father had not grabbed him by the seat of his pants he would have fallen off the sill. It was one of the rare occasions when any of the children were smacked.

Home Leave lasted a year so the children had to go to school. There was a good, Independent Girl's School in Bickley and that was where I was sent. I had to walk to school; there was a shortcut, a footpath running along the railway track, but it didn't seem very short to me. Memories of that year are blurred. My grandparents had bought a car for the family to use, a Ford Anglia, which we all squeezed into, Michael sitting on Mummy's knee in the front – no seat belts then. There was a television, one of the very early ones. It was housed in a walnut cabinet which later became a bedside cupboard. I knew if I hurried home from school I would be in time to watch Andy Pandy so I always hoped the teacher would let the class out quickly so that I would be home in time. The adults thought the exercise was good for me so whatever the weather I had to walk. It seemed a long walk though it can't have been more than twenty minutes.

Jane Moss, who years later became my sister-in-law, was at the same school. She was good at everything and everyone wanted to be her friend. She was kind to me and sometimes she sat next to me at break time. We were all given half-pint bottles of milk to drink, part of the Government Health regime to make sure all children had calcium to build strong bones. I thought I had bones that were quite strong enough but I drank my milk because that was the right thing to do. On Sundays, there was the laundry basket to sort out and be dropped off at Mrs Brigden's and the basket of clean laundry to be collected on the way to church. So many items filled the weekly laundry basket. I sat on the top stair and counted my grandfather's shirt collars – white, stiff and detached from the shirt. There were pillowcases, white damask table napkins, and sheets – all to be counted and written down in a special laundry book and I enjoyed writing them all neatly in the book. When we got to church, Aunty Gwen took Sunday school which I liked.

There was Christmas in England. Aunty Gwen showed David, Andrew and me how to make paper chains. Michael sat and watched. Aunty Gwen thought there was something wrong with Michael because he didn't seem to want to walk or talk and he was two that December. She made poor Wendy take him to see a paediatrician who said there was nothing whatsoever wrong with him, he was just lazy. Kenneth was cross at what he considered was Gwen's intrusion and there was a lot of hissing – my parents never shouted at each other, they just hissed. So Michael sat and watched all the excitement of decorating the tree and hanging up the paper chains. Granny was very busy in the kitchen. All the dried fruit had to be cleaned by covering it with flour and then shaking out the flour, and the weevils, through a sieve, a practice left over from the war years. There were pastry bits left over which I was allowed to use to make my own mince pies, and bowls that the children took turns to scrape and lick.

On Christmas Eve, we four children were bundled into the car. We had a new chauffeur by then called Cable. He replaced Wallington when it was discovered that Wallington and the man at the garage had a good thing going – the car was filled with petrol, the bill was doubled, the two men pocketed half each of the extra money and my grandfather was never the wiser. But one day he became wiser and Wallington was dismissed not to be heard of again. Cable was employed and on Christmas Eve, he was summoned to remove the children. "For goodness sake, get these children out of my hair!" Wendy said. "Take them through the Dartford Tunnel and see if you can find some Christmas lights to show them." Cable quite enjoyed that sort of trip and the four children felt it was one of the highlights of that English Christmas. It snowed – what excitement. There were snowball fights and a snowman, wet gloves and freezing fingers and toes.

Boxing Day was a trip to the circus – a real circus! We went up to Ealing to link up with Aunty Doris, Uncle Oliver and the three boy cousins. Uncle Oliver was a funny man: he always had to go to bed at 9.30 pm so at 9 p.m. whoever was there, he made a cup of tea for and then they all went to bed. Nanny and Molly ran the house. Nanny looked after the children and Molly cooked. Aunty Doris spoke at meetings and did Bible Studies and told me I had to polish my face with a piece of chamois leather to make the skin soft – a bit like polishing the silver only it seemed to be more successful on the silver. Anyway, we all went to the circus together. We had never seen anything like it. I found the clowns really scary, Andrew hid under the seat and David cried. An experience and a memory if not altogether a success.

Much of the time my parents were away preaching in the churches that supported the work of the Missionary Society. Sometimes they came home with surprises. On one trip they stayed in a hotel and brought back little jars – jam for David, honey for Andrew, different jam for Michael and lemon curd for me. They had forgotten I hated lemon curd but I was much too polite to remind them. I hid it under my clothes in a drawer until it went green and then, when I found it green, I put it in the dustbin wrapped up in some old newspaper so that nobody would know. I should have done that in the first place. When they went away Aunty Gwen was left in charge. She must have been exhausted but we loved her. In the spring, there were walks and picnics. One day she took us to Biggin Hill to watch the planes landing at the airstrip there. We were getting out the picnic things when a plane swooped in particularly low. We all fell flat on our faces – I was sure I could feel my hair being blown all over the place by the rush of the wind. I was too scared to look up and wave at the pilot. Anyway, I was distracted by Michael who was knocked over into some nettles and was crying so a dock leaf had to be found to counteract the sting of the nettles. We packed up the picnic, went home and had the picnic in the garden and told our grandparents our adventures.

At Easter, we all decamped to Elmer Sands near Bognor where Aunty Doris had a bungalow with walls that seemed to stretch to accommodate us. The bungalow was made out of two old railway carriages pushed together with various rooms added on. The dining room was one of the carriages with a long table that was able to accommodate all twelve of the family. Aunty Doris had Molly to help her with all the cooking. Near the bungalow was a small hotel where the grandparents stayed. There was a big loft with beds for the seven children. The only access to the loft was a ladder. I hated having to climb up, especially when I got to the top and there was nothing to hold on to but there didn't seem to be an alternative so I gritted my teeth and got on with it. I was the only girl, the eldest at eleven, and I hated having to share with the six noisy boys.

The three cousins and I all had bicycles which we rode around the estate and down to the beach. One day we ventured further afield and were stopped by a policeman who told me I was too wobbly on the bike and that I was not to ride on the main roads. I was so frightened that I was going to be put in prison that I walked all the way home pushing the bike. The boys raced back home with the news that I was going to be arrested. A search party was sent out in the car to look for me but somehow they missed me and I arrived at the bungalow very tired, very frightened and very cross. I put the bike in the shed and there it stayed. Molly was very understanding, gave me a hug and a hot drink and told me that the police were too busy chasing criminals to worry about one little girl.

On one wonderful day, my grandparents took me out for a treat all by myself. My parents were away for the day so there was nobody there to put a spanner in the works. We had tea in a little tea shop and then my grandfather bought me a teddy bear to replace Monday. He was a beautiful bear and I couldn't believe he belonged to me. We went back to the bungalow and found my parents had returned so I showed the bear to Mummy who was not at all pleased. "You should never have bought her that bear," she told her father. "Rachel doesn't need special treatment and you are in danger of spoiling her. I really don't want her to have the bear. I would like you to take it back where it came from. Presents are for birthdays and Christmas." So the bear was returned and I cried quietly into my pillow. I certainly didn't want to be told not to make a fuss nor to be teased by the boys – all very real possibilities.

Before we had come home on leave, Granny and Aunty Gwen had a chat about meals. They had decided that they could not be responsible for a midday meal every day so they arranged with the local hotel, a five-minute walk down the road, that we would all eat lunch there. One of the residents in the hotel was a man called Mr Cohen. Aunty Gwen sat me down with my brothers and explained to us that he had fought in the war and had lost both a leg and an eye. He now had a wooden replacement leg which was attached by straps to his thigh, and a false eye which neither moved nor blinked giving Mr Cohen a peculiar stare. The boys lost interest at that point only asking if Mr Cohen had a gun. "No!" said Aunty Gwen. Aunty Gwen told me – I was really very nosy – that at night he took off his leg and took out his eye. I was horrified – poor Mrs

Cohen! How did she feel every night when bits of Mr Cohen sat on the chair or in a tooth mug by the bed? Aunty Gwen told me that I was not to ask Mr Cohen. Every lunchtime I watched Mr Cohen out of the corner of my eye hoping no bits would fall off. He seemed to manage all right using his walking stick and smiling at me when I smiled at him. Mrs Cohen had died and I wasn't surprised – I thought it must have been hard for her to have had to live with a husband who had to take himself apart at bedtime. No wonder she had died!

Although the family was based in Bickley, there were trips to other places. Every summer there was a big Christian gathering in Wales at a school in Abergele. Daddy was one of the speakers so the whole family went for a week. There were all sorts of different meetings with activities laid on for us children, communal meals and excursions to interesting places nearby. One Sunday morning I woke up very early. I was sharing a room with the three boys and I didn't want to wake them so I got out a new sewing kit I had been given. It contained all the pieces to sew together to make a felt dog. I read the instructions very carefully first and worked out which bit went where. The pack had a needle and thread included so there was no reason why I could not start. I was well on the way to completion by the time Mummy came into the room to get us up for breakfast. I was very proud of the progress I had made and was about to show Mummy who was looking at me in horror. "What are you doing?" she asked. "You know we don't sew on a Sunday. Put that away at once!" I bundled all the pieces of the half-sewn dog back into the pack. I never touched it again. Was it really such a sin for a little girl to sew her dog at 6.30 on a Sunday morning? There was a rigidity about their faith that was hard to fathom. Perhaps the lack of grey areas made it easier to live up to the standards required to be a Christian. For me, it was a minefield.

The summer passed. There was a visit to the zoo. Aunty Gwen knew the man who was in charge of London Zoo. He was called Mr Cansdale and Aunty Gwen rang him up and told him she was coming up to visit the zoo with her nephews and niece from Africa. He said they would be used to monkeys so they could have tea with the chimpanzees! The boys were very excited; I wasn't too sure. I knew how vicious chimpanzees could be if they didn't get their own way. Anyway, Cable was called to drive us up to London where the zoo was and off we went. It was a wonderful day. David wanted to see everything all at once; Andrew wanted to spend hours in the snake house – he said they had to be very quiet and wait until the snakes shed their skins. Aunty Gwen said there really wasn't time to wait for that as they only shed skins once a year. They thought Andrew was going to have a meltdown, so he was distracted by a promise to ride an elephant and that seemed to do the trick. Michael sat quietly in his pushchair absorbing everything. I flatly refused to go on the special chair on the back of the elephant. I felt it was far too far off the ground so I waited with Aunty Gwen and Michael while the other two waved and shouted and got so excited I thought they might fall out. So did Aunty Gwen, whose voice got quite cross when she called out to them to behave!

After lunch, we met important Mr Cansdale and were taken to the chimpanzee enclosure where there were little chairs and a table with cups and saucers laid out. I was greatly relieved to discover that we were to watch through glass rather than share the tea party. I couldn't believe the way the chimpanzees held the cups and drank from them. They were a lot better at it than Michael! Eventually, goodbyes and thank yous were said and Cable was there to take us home. When we got back to Tomatin, David rushed into the house wanting to tell his parents all that they had been doing. Andrew was found sitting on the stairs. When Wendy asked him whatever was the matter he replied, "David has told you everything and there is nothing left for me to tell!" Poor Andrew! That was the story of his life. David was always one step ahead of him. Ultimately, that led to his emigration and to settling in New Zealand where he could, at last, be his own person.

The autumn came and it was time to pack up. Leave had come to an end and the family packed their bags ready to go back to Africa for another four-year tour. We were to be posted to Burundi to the Mission station called Matana – a hospital, a school and of course a church. There were to be two other mission houses there – one was for the two missionary nurses and the other for a widow and her daughter who were involved in translation work. The daughter was at this time, the translator while her mother was writing a story. I was to spend many tedious hours listening to her story which I was too polite to criticise though my stifled yawns should have been enough to make my reaction quite clear. The name of this elderly lady was Mrs Guillebaud, always referred to as Mrs G. She was a formidable woman with a heart of gold but she had a way of dictating to Wendy what she thought would be best for her. Like the time she found pilchards on offer and reduced Mummy to tears of frustration when she presented her with 24 tins and the bill. "But we don't even like pilchards!" wailed poor Mummy. The best thing about the Guillebauds, I was to discover, was that they belonged to a book club and each month new books were sent out. They were novels and neither of my parents had time to censor my reading.

The family were to sail back to Africa, the reasoning being that they needed a rest after the demands of constant preaching while on Leave. So, down to Tilbury dock we went and embarked on the ship that was to be home for the next month. Aunty Gwen came to see us off as did my grandparents.

There were hugs and tears. I had thought Aunty Gwen was coming too. She must have been equally exhausted from having a family to look after for a year, and I was devastated when I realised she was getting off the boat. The gangway was hauled up and the family stood at the rails waving at the three figures getting smaller and smaller as the ship chugged its way out to sea. I cried, first with proper tears and then for a long time with inside tears. (All my life I have had to learn to cry inside. I learnt very young that people get fed up with outside tears.)

Once we had all settled in we had a lot of fun on board. There was the fun of reaching different ports. At the Suez Canal there was the gilli-gilli man with his basket of tiny, fluffy yellow chicks; were they the same as the ones I remembered from the last trip? There were small boats that crowded the side of the ship. Mummy bought a big-brimmed straw hat which she wore all through that tour. When the boat crossed the line (the equator), there was a party with a lot of splashing in the pool and cream cakes being thrown in peoples' faces. I liked watching from a safe distance.

The highlight, at least for the missionary families on board, was the fancy dress competition. My father was delighted to be able to use his creative skills, this was a chance to show just what he could do. I wanted to go as a princess but my father was having none of it – I was to go as a candle! My head was to be the flame with a flame mask; my body was to be the candle itself so I would be wrapped around with a white sheet, and around my knees would be the candle holder, a complicated construction consisting of a cardboard circle surrounded by a frame with a handle all fixed round my knees. I stood in the cabin for hours while Daddy cut and pinned, muttered and adjusted, and stuck, pinned and painted. The result was magnificent. Daddy sat back on the bunk and admired his handiwork. The boys were dressed as very convincing pirates with patches and swords – David nearly decapitated Michael whose wails merely added to the chaos. Michael had beautiful blond, curly hair and made a most convincing girl. The family were ready to go. The boys were ushered out into the corridor but now there was a crisis – I couldn't fit through the door! The impressive candle holder was too wide and anyway, my knees were pinned together so I was barely able to shuffle. However, nothing daunted my father, so he carefully took it apart and carried it up to the deck where it was reassembled around me. To my father's great delight, I won a prize and to my great relief, I was allowed to climb out of the contraption. Michael also won a prize. David and Andrew had a sword fight and had to be hastily removed from the scene amid much cheering and laughter.

We arrived in the November heat of Mombasa and boarded the train to Nairobi and then on to Kampala. It was a magical three-day journey. Before every meal, a waiter dressed in a white kanzu and a red fez walked the length of the train playing a hand-held xylophone to call the passengers to the dining car. There were white cloths on the tables and white plates with cutlery that looked like silver and starched white napkins. Even my brothers were awed into good behaviour! When we got back to our cabins the top bunks had been pulled down and proper beds had been made. The movement of the train lulled each one to sleep.

During breakfast, the beds were put away and the days were spent looking for game through the windows, playing games, drawing and colouring and reading. Time seemed to pass in no time at all. The train stopped at stations with exotic-sounding names like Timau, Tororo, Nakuru and Jinja. It was to be the first of many train journeys but far more luxurious than the ones that were to follow. On future journeys, for economy's sake, only the evening meal and breakfast were paid for and sleeping bags were unrolled with a bundle of clothes for pillows rather than the luxury of bedding rolls.

When the family reached Kampala there was a taxi up to the CMS Guest House and hot days were spent trailing around the shops. A new car, an Opal Estate, was waiting for collection and a roof rack was fitted. The luggage was piled on top and inside the car and the family squeezed in somehow. They set off on the three-daylong journey to Matana. The roads were red earth so following any other vehicle resulted in clouds of red dust, windows being rapidly wound up and Kenneth taking his family's lives in his hands as he blindly overtook, unable to see any oncoming traffic through the dust clouds. Wendy arrived at each night stop covered in dust and stressed beyond measure!

We washed our hair in basins in our rooms – no running water but water scooped out of the old oil drums placed in strategic places under guttering off the roof to catch any rain. The water was so soft only the smallest blob of shampoo was necessary. Kenneth said soap and water was quite enough, shampoo was all a lot of sham and a bit of poo! I loved the sudsy shampoo snow cap until it dripped into my eyes. The water was always red from the dust.

Each morning preparations were made for the day in the car. There were rolls filled with cold baked beans, Marmite or hard-boiled eggs for picnics on the journey. One picnic was hijacked by a swarm of bees. Someone had disturbed their hive and they swarmed all over the family. Wendy's long hair acted as a trap and she ran about slapping at her head; Kenneth had no hair so the bees stung his scalp; David and Andrew joined the general excitement running about and screaming; Michael sat stolidly on the rug and watched; I moved out of the way and watched. Only Michael and I avoided being stung.

There are advantages to sitting still. Eventually, the journey was resumed with everyone feeling the worse for wear.

At each stop, the family were welcomed into a missionary home. Visitors were rare and brought news from other missionaries and my father was a particularly welcome guest. There were always problems to be aired and advice to be sought and Kenneth was wise and a very good listener. There was always one more tangle to be untangled just as the family had been shoehorned into the car so there we sat, hot and cross and waiting. I seemed to be forever waiting so I made sure I had a book to read. It was the start of a life-long habit and to this day I try never to leave the house without a book secreted somewhere about me.

The last stop and the most southern Mission station in Burundi was Matana. It was to be our home for the next six years. There was a year's break when I was 16 while the family covered for another doctor who went on Leave from a Mission station in Rwanda, and then Kenneth went back alone to Matana for a year while the family stayed in England. Wendy was needed there to settle the boys into school and to provide a home while Kenneth completed his work in Africa. But that was years in the future.

Now it is 1952 and time to settle down in Matana and get the children off to school. Let's have a closer look at the place where I was to spend my teenage years. The house was a bungalow with a tin roof so that when it rained the drum roll on the roof prevented easy conversation. There was a covered entrance porch and then you walked straight into the sitting room with a large bay window, an open fireplace and an area for a dining room table and chairs. It was a beautiful table made out of a single plank of wood, highly polished with a beeswax polish Wendy made from the wax from a local hive. It was a rather dark room but it did have linoleum flooring which Wendy's father had shipped out from his firm in England. I was prone to falling at that time, unsteady on my feet but determined to do without any aids so rather than let me fall on concrete, it was decided to ship out the linoleum from my grandfather's factory. It was the only Mission house to have floor covering; all the others had red, polished concrete. I thought that made us quite a posh family! Each bedroom branched off from the big family room. I had my own room. It had a nice window, a dressing table and a basin and a jug of water which stood on top. One corner of the room had a rail and a curtain which hid my dresses.

Wendy had found dresses which she thought suited me so she had bought four of the same style but in different colour combinations – one blue, one mauve, one pink and one green. To be on the safe side and to accommodate my inevitable growth, she had bought them in different sizes, but with the same pattern and the same colours. When you are 14 it is hard to still have the same style and pattern that you were wearing when you were 10, but that did not seem to occur to my thrifty, bewildered mother, who seemed out of her depth in so many areas of her life.

Looking back as an adult, it seems that, for Wendy, it was a matter of survival, of "doing God's will" in such an alien environment. She had to let her hair grow as there was no one to cut it. She wound it around a shoelace into a sort of sausage bun at the nape of her neck! No fashion in darkest Africa! She helped with the hospital accounts and at the end of each month she shut herself in her bedroom, emptied bags of money all over her bed and counted it out into piles. Amounts were entered into a large ledger and there was a lot of muttering and recounting. Woe betide any child who interrupted the counting! It seemed that she was in a constant state of anxiety. The whole African experience seemed to take her right out of her comfort zone and in the years after she left she never expressed any desire to go back, nor did she ever talk about friends she had made beyond other missionaries. However, she did all that was required of her, fully convinced that she was in the right place and determined to support Kenneth in every way. She did manage a little French which helped as Kenneth could not go much beyond "Bonjour" on a good day – paralysed on a bad one!

There was plenty of help in the house but Wendy wanted to be sure I learnt to pull my weight too, so after breakfast, I was expected to help make the beds. Girls made beds, boys played outside. The loo was housed in a small hut away from the house just as it had been in Kigeme - a "long drop" facing away from the house and again with no door and only a piece of string hanging from a post. Nobody wanted to venture out in the middle of the night so under each person's bed was a potty which was emptied each morning by the lovely girl who helped in the house.

Each morning, after bed-making, Wendy installed herself in the walk-in store. It had sacks of flour and sugar and endless tins – tins of margarine and dried milk, baked beans, sardines, Mrs G's pilchards, fruit, custard powder, even the luxury of Kenya butter in a tin – everything that could be tinned seemed to live in the store. Milk was delivered every morning and Wendy had a special thermometer-type gadget that measured whether the milk had been diluted, usually with cows' urine. The milk was boiled and left to cool and then the thick cream was scooped off the top and churned into butter – not nearly as nice as the Kenya butter! Wendy kept chickens so there were always eggs. When the chicken had served its time, the cook wrung its neck ready for the pot. My brothers insisted on being there to watch the poor dead chicken run its last race around the yard, its head hanging limp.

The cook would come daily for his instructions. Wendy would suggest the meals for the day and hand out any necessary ingredients all carefully weighed out. There was always a cake or biscuits for tea. On one memorable occasion, Aunty Gwen sent out a sheet of edible rice paper on which she had drawn circles with pictures and the names of each member of the family. Wendy cut out the circles and used them as the base for biscuits. When it came to tea time each person had their own biscuit with their name and a special message from Aunty Gwen. What magic! How did Aunty Gwen post them without them breaking? Well, Aunty Gwen could do anything!

There were oranges in the orchard and some enterprising previous missionaries had planted Seville oranges as well as ordinary eaters so once a year it was marmalade making time. Wendy had a recipe from the Chivers factory and that entailed chopping up the peel by hand so I was roped in to chop. I got very bored. Lemons were plentiful so "waste not, want not" and we all set about making juice. We set up a chain with somebody cutting – David cut his finger and there was a plaster crisis with David screaming convincingly – somebody pushing down the handle on the special squeezing machine that had been brought over from England, and somebody bottling the juice. Citric acid was always added as a preservative.

So what else did I do to fill my days? Mrs G's books from England provided an escape but there were only two a month so they had to be made to last as long as possible so reading was kept to the afternoon. Once the chores had been done I would wander down to the church where there was an out-of-tune organ installed. I would play hymn tunes and practise the music I brought home from school. I wasn't very good and never progressed beyond Grade Five but it was fun pushing and pulling the stops though it didn't seem to make much difference whether they were in or out! There was always embroidery on the go or tapestry and there were books with pictures to be painted – be careful not to go over the lines! I did not inherit my father's gift of drawing or painting so nothing original was ever created. When I was 15, Mummy gave me a length of material and a dress pattern and I made my first dress which was a great success. "Follow the instructions," was Mummy's advice – she had never made a dress herself – so that was what I did. Wendy had an old Singer sewing machine, a turn-the-handle model, on which she had made the boys' shirts and shorts incurring sleepless nights worrying as to how to fit the gusset in the shorts! But I wasn't making shorts with problematic gussets and problems with setting in zips and fitting in sleeves were beyond my mother's experience so I followed the pattern instructions and hoped for the best.

Wearing the first dress I made for myself, aged 16

Sometimes I went with my mother to visit African families but that was rare, and there were invitations to tea with the two white missionary nurses or to the Guillebauds. I had learnt to ride a bike so there were bike rides around the mission compound and the dreaded Sunday walk. This was a family affair and the walk took the family down into the valley where there was a small lake and a vegetable garden. The path was narrow accommodating two abreast; the three boys ran on ahead, then came my parents arm in arm, heads together talking over the week's events; I followed two or three paces behind always "keeping up". There were meant to be fish in the lake. Michael says they could be seen swimming around. Kenneth wanted to catch some so a net was stretched out in the water and he detonated some gunpowder which killed all the fish, blew a hole in the net and still there didn't seem to be any fish on the table. But perhaps that is an apocryphal tale! However, there were always fresh vegetables and at least the walk was only once a week.

We all went to church on Sundays carrying our chairs with us as most of the congregation sat on benches or on the floor. We were the only white people many of the children had ever seen and my longish hair was a source of great interest. As I sat waiting for the service to start I was subjected to frequent hair-stroking by the children. Wendy played the organ and the minister banged the drum. He led the singing and the drum kept Wendy and all the congregation in time, more or less. The service lasted for anything up to three hours – after all, most of the congregation had a long walk to get to church so they wanted their money's worth. For us, it was all very boring – except for the day when suddenly the doors were locked, and the cry, "A rabid dog!" went up. Somebody produced a gun from somewhere and the dog was shot but not before it had bitten somebody. The man was admitted to the hospital and

Kenneth came home distraught at the lack of help he could give the patient who had a raging thirst and a phobia of water – the two symptoms of rabies. Death was merciful on that occasion.

Every year the family took off for their annual four-week holiday. Most years the month was spent with other families by a lake at a place called Nabagubo in Uganda. Each family had their own house built in a semi-circle facing the lake. The houses were fairly primitive with very basic furniture, beds with a rope base covered with a lumpy mattress, and an outside loo. There were kitchens at the back of the houses and most families brought their house staff with them. Each house had a veranda where adults could sit and watch the children. There were canoes to paddle, swimming and the most amazing butterflies to catch. There were monkeys in the trees which were a constant threat to the bananas left in bowls on tables and quickly not left in bowls but hidden away from thieving fingers.

On one of the holidays, I found a baby monkey which had somehow gotten separated from the rest of the troop. I rescued it, fed it and kept it wrapped up in a towel and carried it around in my arms for the rest of the holiday. I was brokenhearted when at the end of the holiday the monkey had to be returned to the wild but there was no way Mummy was going to allow me to take it home. Two weeks were quite long enough to have that addition to the family!

Missionaries don't do holidays without some spiritual input and so time each day was set aside for Kenneth to do his preparation for the Bible Study he gave each morning for the other missionaries. It was an adults-only meeting so the children had to keep out of the way and find quiet things to do. One of the quiet things was pinning out the butterflies on a board. We had butterfly nets made out of old mosquito nets attached to wireframes and we would catch the butterflies and kill them with a whiff of chloroform. It was surprising that none of us were put to sleep too! They were the most beautifully coloured butterflies of all sizes and, pinned out on boards, they were framed and hung on bedroom walls.

There were board games to play and the group of boys spent many happy hours playing with dinky cars in the grey sand on the edge of the lake. There were the dug-out canoes to paddle and fun to be had racing them. Children fell out and were hauled in again lest the crocodiles in the lake took a fancy to them. When I was 17, Anthony came to stay for a week. We had been keeping up a desultory correspondence while he was teaching at Turi school. Now it was time to see whether this was to go on or not. Anthony's problem was that he had been teaching with Tim and a nice girl called Pat. Both Anthony and Tim fancied Pat and were waiting to see which one she would choose. Anthony thought it was sensible to have two strings to his bow so he came to stay with us. He held my hand and I thought I was in heaven – the missionaries weren't too sure this was suitable behaviour so they had a chat, prayed and decided that young love could have its way, provided they kept a strict eye on the couple. Pat chose Tim and married him; eventually, I married Anthony.

There were two memorable holidays when the family went to Mombasa. We rented a house on the south coast for one holiday and on the north coast for the second time. On both occasions, we linked up with other missionary families. We spent hours searching for shells on the reef which could be accessed on foot when the tide was out. We spent one day on a beach where there was a break in the reef so the waves were big enough for surfing. I thought I was brave enough to swim but I got bundled by a particularly big wave, thought I was going to drown and, when I could eventually get to my feet, vowed I would only ever swim in calm water, a vow I adhered to all my life! We went into Mombasa using the ferry to get across to the island on which the town is built. I loved the ferry with its hustle and bustle, peanuts in paper cones, the smell of fish, the huge bunches of bananas and the baskets of mangoes. We visited the Old Town with its old fort and narrow passageways where old Arab men squatted outside dark little shops often smoking long pipes. When I revisited as an adult, I found a blackened copper tray which an old man fished out from under his bed in the dark interior of his "duka". I bought and cleaned it, first with lemon juice and then with copper cleaner. It now hangs on the wall in our sitting room.

One holiday was spent in a house just north of the ferry where we could sit on the veranda and watch the ferry plying its trade and the huge Liners coming into the port in Mombasa. The boats came close enough to see the passengers on board, lounging in deck chairs or leaning on the rail and waving. At night the ship was moored in the harbour, lit up like a small town. I remembered our journey out on a similar boat, a world away from the reality of ordinary life.

The holidays were memorable but so were the occasional family days out from home. They were few and far between as it was seldom that Kenneth could be spared but perhaps all the more special because of their rarity. The favourite place to go was the source of the Nile which was supposed to be in the hills about an hour's drive from the mission station. Part of the fun was of course the picnic lunch. The cook made fresh rolls which were wrapped in a tea towel. There were hard-boiled eggs, cold baked beans, and sardines as fillings. There were always homemade biscuits and finger bananas and, in season, mangoes despite their messiness. One time when all the plans were made and the picnic packed Wendy cried off at the last minute with a headache but Kenneth was determined to go on with the plan so he took the children by himself. I was put in charge of managing the food. Even in those days, I was frightened of getting it wrong somehow and the memory of that picnic still tightens my tummy muscles with anxiety. Nothing was ever so secure without my mother at the helm.

Sometimes the expeditions were to Bujumbura which was the capital centre for Burundi. On the way there the family often stopped at an American mission station. The main house was situated on a hill with the most magnificent view out over the rolling hillside. It was my first experience of understanding what was meant by "the view", a phrase I had read but never comprehended. American missionaries lived a much grander lifestyle than their British counterparts. They had enormous fridges and ate jelly with their meat and in this particular house, they had a xylophone which the lady missionary played. The keyboard was the size of a piano keyboard and I had neither seen nor heard anything like it. What with the view, the xylophone and the jelly with the meat, it was definitely a never-to-be-forgotten memory.

Shopping in Bujumbura was a nightmare! It was hot and most of the time, we children had to wait in the car while our parents visited shop after shop trying to stock up for the next three months. I made sure I was never without a book to read but the boys were bored and quarrelsome and Daddy and Mummy were hot and hassled! There was usually a welcome break for lunch with a Scandinavian missionary family – they had jelly with their meat too but they also had ice cream and air-conditioning.

It was all quite restricting for a teenage girl – none of the entertainment enjoyed by my peers. I had never been to the cinema until one of the staff at school discovered this horrific fact when I was 16 and took me to see "Gigi" in Nairobi. But that is another story. I did manage to get hold of some make-up at school which I took home and applied, with little expertise and much enthusiasm, one evening by the light of a hurricane lamp. Admittedly the result was hardly an improvement. I was sent straight back to my room to wash it off. In my parents' eyes make-up was the tool of the Devil and certainly not to be used by good Christian girls. At that stage in my life, I wasn't sure I wanted to be a good Christian girl anyway but there wasn't much opportunity to rebel so I didn't bother.

We did have a croquet set in the garden which I quite enjoyed especially when I was joined by a nice African boy. Where he appeared from is a mystery but whenever I went out to practice he appeared. He was better at it than I was and we laughed a lot at our attempts to knock each other out of the way of the hoops. Mummy took me aside one day and explained that he was not a suitable companion, white girls did not play with black boys, and somebody must have warned him too because he did not appear again and I couldn't be bothered to play croquet any more.

SCHOOL DAYS

The Limuru Girls School brown school uniform was laid out on the bed. There were brown tunics and cream shirts; brown pullovers and huge brown knickers; a brown girdle tied like a tie was worn round the waist; brown socks and lace-up shoes; a brown blazer and hat completed the outfit. Of course, there were socks to name and a games kit, towels, swimming costumes and even hankies! This move to secondary school should have been exciting but it didn't feel like that. Everything was packed into my trunk – everything except my night things for the journey. These were squashed into an oblong zip-up bag known as "Rachel's sausage" which I silently loathed but which accompanied me for the six years I spent at Limuru Girls' School.

At school at Limuru - the dreaded brown uniform.

There were three private secondary girls' schools in or near Nairobi – Limuru which was the posh one designed to turn out young ladies, small in that there were only 150 girls, with a charismatic headmistress called Miss Fisher who went on to become Head of Wycombe Abbey Girls' School. Then there was The Kenya High – more about that one later. Lastly, there was The Convent which was Roman Catholic and much like Limuru.

The long journey ate into the holidays. There were the three days in the car with nights spent at Mission Stations on the way and then there was the overnight train journey. The train was quite fun especially when the boys' schools were going back at the same time! Parents bought meal vouchers for their children and, if one was really lucky, there was even a bedding voucher. If there was a bedding voucher, while they were all in the dining car for dinner, one of the African attendants put down the bunk and unrolled sheets, blankets and a towel. What luxury and what luxury the meals were too. An attendant would walk the length of the train playing a xylophone gong and everyone crowded into the dining car to be served a wonderful meal with white tablecloths and waiters. I didn't often have the joy of a bedding roll as her "sausage" was designed to accommodate a sleeping bag and that was considered quite sufficient for an 11-year-old.

For the first year at Limuru, the school was moved into Nairobi as it was considered far too dangerous to be out of town with the Mau-Mau running amok. The school was allocated two boarding houses at the Kenya High School. This school was much bigger, with some 600 pupils, the majority of whom were boarders. There must have been eight houses built in a semicircle with Mitchel and Mortimer occupied by Limuru girls. How miserable I was. My dormitory was in Mitchel House and was as far from the teaching block as it was possible to be. Every morning, I filled my bag with all that was necessary for the day, nothing must be forgotten because the trek back was too far and took too long for me to manage. The other girls were able to run back at lunchtime and stock up for the afternoon but it was not feasible for me so a day's packing was essential. The bag was heavy; the journey from house to the classroom never grew any shorter. The games fields were even further to walk. Although I was not able to participate in tennis or hockey there was a wall for tennis practice and a basket for netball practice and I was encouraged to use both while the others ran about waving hockey sticks and tennis rackets.

Those early days were mostly a blur, to be endured because there was no escape. I did not seem to have any special friends. Survival was all that mattered. But even relocation of schools must come to an end and, after three terms, the school moved back to its grounds in Limuru. There was barbed wire fencing to protect the inmates and the army sent soldiers to guard the girls. In retrospect, it seems that it should have been the other way around! It was the soldiers who needed protection.

The main building of the school was a three-storey house. The ground floor had two dormitories, washrooms, and a large common room with a big fireplace at one end – haunted – and then a dining room extension. The second storey was all dormitories with a sick room and Matrons' rooms. The top storey was for the prefects and had twin rooms – and a very convenient fire escape. In order to protect the girls from a Mau-Mau attack, hockey sticks and tins of pepper were issued to everyone. The instructions were, "In the case of an attack every girl must run to the second storey and stand ready to hit the advancing Mau-Mau on the head with the hockey stick having first blinded them by throwing the pepper in their eyes!" I was put into one of the ground floor dormitories with 15 and

16-year-old girls despite the fact that I was only 12 – the stairs were deemed to be too much for me. I stowed my hockey stick under my bed and put the tin of pepper into my locker with my bible – a better weapon in the case of an emergency I felt. The dormitory windows looked out onto the school library and that was given over to the army as their recreation room. How convenient! Lights went out, windows opened and, despite the bars on the windows to protect the inmates, conversations were conducted in whispers. Both parties enjoyed this enormously. What more could a young man want than a pretty girl in her pyjamas however inaccessible and there were many promises made and unfulfilled!

After a year the danger was over, the army left and the barbed wire fencing was removed. A nice girl called Anna Boddy arrived from Tanzania and she and I became friends, not particularly good friends but friends nonetheless. Anna slept on the second floor but I was moved out of the room I had been in into a cubbyhole under the stairs. There was just room for a bed – you could just sit up without banging your head on the underside of the stairs – and a bedside locker. There was a small window and I loved it. I devoured book after book; nobody bothered to check whether I was reading by torchlight after lights out and new torch batteries were readily available at the school Tuck Shop. "Gone with the Wind" with steady Ashley and flamboyant, heroic Rett Butler will forever live in my memory. Books were my introduction to the wider world. They provided much of my sex education and I began to realise that there was a lot more to explore beyond the narrow missionary world I inhabited with my parents.

Half-term outings also broadened my horizons. I went to stay with a friend called Vicky who lived on a farm near Kericho – I was mortified when Mummy pronounced it to rhyme with Jericho – where they had horses and a drinks party (on a Sunday!) instead of church! I helped hand round drinks and canapés and listened to the noise levels rising and felt increasingly out of my depth so I crept away. Sometime later Vicky found me on the veranda reading and ushered me back into the dining room for a very late lunch.

The other feature of that half-term was horse riding which was alarming, to say the least. I didn't have any trousers of any sort – of course I didn't; missionaries didn't wear trousers – so I was squeezed into a pair of Vicky's. My weight was always a problem, I never seemed to manage to lose enough so Vicky's trousers were squeezingly tight. The horse was enormous. I really wasn't sure I could be polite enough to allow myself to be hoisted up onto its back. Don't forget, I was wearing a calliper on one leg and was only about three years out of my arm splint so I was quite hampered physically, let alone terrified. But my mother had said I had to do everything and to never make polio an excuse so I bravely clutched the reins and prayed I wouldn't fall off. God wasn't listening. The horse started to trot and I fell off! I picked myself up, was dusted down by concerned adults, checked surreptitiously that the very tight trousers hadn't split – they hadn't, mercifully – and I was helped on again, "Best to get straight back on or you will never learn to ride!" I did get back on and I did manage a short ride, holding on, terrified but not bothering to pray as God was obviously having a day off. I have never been on a horse since. I came away quite convinced that Vicky and her family were destined for Hell. Was it possible to go to Heaven and have a drinks party on a Sunday? It was all a puzzle and the worst bit was that Vicky's world seemed so much more interesting than my missionary world. My education was sadly lacking when it came to the ways of the world. Anyway better not to worry about these things at the moment.

But there were other, less confusing half-terms. There

was a kind doctor and his wife who scooped up a lot of the missionary children for exeats. They had a big house on the outskirts of Nairobi. There was a large garden with a stream at the bottom and plenty of rooms to sleep extras. They had three children of their own, all three adopted – Nigel, Jenny and Anna. Jenny was at the High School and Nigel at the big Boys' School but half-terms were all at the same time so there was always a house full of children. I went there for the weekend of the Queen's Coronation. The Hindley boys were there too and I scrambled about on the banks of the stream with Anthony and Peter and got wet and took no notice of the Coronation. They had Coronation chicken for lunch. The recipe had been published before the great day so that the British all over the world could celebrate together.

And the third memorable outing was to the Nairobi Agricultural Show. The whole school was transported by bus. We were allowed to wear home clothes so the senior girls looked magnificent in beautiful dresses and carefully applied makeup. I wondered if I would ever manage to look like that. I never have! Once at the showground we were free to enjoy ourselves so, armed with a packed lunch, we scattered. The older girls had pre-arranged assignations. Anna and I wandered around looking at prize animals and interesting stalls. Then we settled on seats surrounding the show ring and watched the parades of cows, pigs and sheep, the horses and finally the dogs.

Many years later, when Anthony and I were living in Nakuru, we had a very beautiful Dalmatian which we were asked to show. Anthony wasn't very keen on the idea but I was full of enthusiasm. I coerced Anthony into helping me get George into the bath to give him a good shampoo with a cube of blue dye in the water to make his white even whiter against his black spots. We took him down to Nairobi to the Show where I delivered my final blow, "I can't possibly take him into the ring. I'm seven months pregnant and far too enormous to be seen walking around the ring. You'll have to take him!" Poor Anthony protested loudly but I was having none of it; we had bathed him and scrubbed him, brushed him and polished him "Just walk around nicely and when the judge comes to do a close inspection, make him stand while you hold out his tail. I've seen people do that in pictures in books. You'll be fine!" He was fine and George won second prize! Not long after poor George dropped down dead. Anthony was very relieved not to have to fall in with any more of my good ideas, though they did make life more interesting!

But all that was years in the future. During my time at Limuru the headmistress was a very imposing woman called Miss Fisher; she was the niece of the Archbishop of Canterbury, Dr Fisher. Miss Fisher was a tall, slim woman; she always wore her gown and strode about the school with her hands behind her back and her black gown billowing out like a witch's cloak. Everyone was terrified of her. I did not behave very well to begin with at Limuru – I didn't know how to behave in such a different environment. I didn't know how to make friends so being naughty at least meant I was noticed. I was rude to the prefects who gave me lines, "Empty pitchers make the most noise" to be written out 200 times! At least I never forgot them!

There was a school ghost who was purported to live in the library. I was sleeping in a dormitory at one end of a long corridor; the other end had the bathrooms on one side and the library on the opposite side of the corridor. I persuaded my friend, Anna, to creep along the passage with me and look into the library to see if the ghost was really there. It just so happened that the school matron rounded the corner at the end of the corridor as the girls were creeping along so she followed them to see what they were up to. Anna and I got to the door of the library. Matron was close behind us. Anna opened the door slowly, slowly. We slipped into the room. At the other end of the room, we saw a tall figure in white. We tumbled out of the room, terrified, and scooted back to bed our hearts racing, convinced we had seen the school ghost. Matron smiled as she looked at her reflection in the mirror at the far end of the library. A fright is often more effective than punishment. Nothing would get Anna and me out of bed in the night again.

There was a craze for keeping white mice. The mice were meant to be kept in the science lab. and could be visited at appropriate times but they were very sweet and they got lonely in their cages so some of the girls, me included, carried the mice around with us secreted up our jumper sleeves. The mice, however, were not always cooperative and did not stay put but ran about all over the place – up and down sleeves, round necks, down fronts, round waists, tickling and often in grave danger of being either sat on or discovered. In the classroom, they were safer in the desks so I surreptitiously transferred my mouse to my desk. The desks were old-fashioned with a lid and a hole for an inkwell. The inkwells were filled with ink once a week. For some reason the inkwell on my desk had not been returned, leaving a hole. The class was quiet; I was busy trying, and failing, to work out a maths problem; the teacher was handing back exercise books. When she reached my desk she dropped all the remaining books and shrieked. I knew I was bad at maths but I didn't think I was that bad! It took me a minute to realise that my mouse had popped up through the inkwell hole and was sitting up viewing the room. The mouse was returned to its cage. I was given a detention and an Order Mark. Order Marks were only handed out for really bad offences and often resulted in a visit to the headmistress – a situation to be avoided.

In the wet season, April-June, it was cold so the classrooms were heated with wood fires. Baskets of wood were filled each day and the fires were kept burning all morning and all afternoon if there were afternoon lessons. At break time there were often slices of bread to feed hungry girls. This bread was meant to be eaten in the dining room but it was much nicer to smuggle it out tucked under a jersey and toast it on the end of a ruler over the classroom fire. The rulers got burnt, and skirts were stained with grease marks from the dripping melted butter but reprimands were met with wide-eyed innocence and strong denials despite the evidence.

Rudeness, burnt rulers, white mice, Order Marks – this could not go on. Miss Fisher summoned me. "The trouble with you, young lady, is that you have not got enough to do. I want you to produce a class play which will be performed in front of the whole school at the end of term. Now go and use your time more profitably." I went and found a modern version of the Nativity play, its name is lost in the mists of time. I managed to get the class "cool gang" on side. They rehearsed, I stayed out of trouble, had sleepless nights – no time for ghost hunting – coerced the drama teacher into helping with costumes, gave the best parts to the cool gang and by the end of term we were ready. We performed our play on the last afternoon of the term. It was a great success and Miss Fisher was quietly relieved she had managed to get me back on track. What a wise woman she was!

Classes were small. Bright girls did Latin, others did cookery; I did Latin and wished I could do cookery. English was my favourite subject taught first by Mrs Robertson and then by Miss Stewart. Miss Stewart was young and pretty with lots of blonde hair, good at tennis and easy on the eye, looking for a more exciting life than England had offered. The local farmers vied for her attention. She was dropped off in the evenings by a dashing young man and fond farewells were said in the car just under the dormitory windows. The girls hung out to get the best view. Nobody wanted to interrupt the goodnight kisses so they kept mousey quiet until she got out of the car but then, "Goodnight Miss Stewart!" The following morning Miss Fisher included in morning assembly a tirade on thoughtless behaviour. Miss Stewart got engaged to the man in the car and the school chapel choir was asked to sing at her wedding. The choir wore red robes with white ruffs and underneath we tied sponge bags to our waists. After the service, we went to the reception and handed round plates of food. We smuggled as much as we could into the sponge bag to take back to school to share with friends.

Miss Stewart was not the only member of staff to request the choir to sing at their wedding. Miss Watson also got married. Miss Watson taught Latin and was the choir mistress. She was tiny and well into her forties and was to marry a man of over six feet tall. I liked Miss Watson. I was good at Latin and I liked singing in the choir One of the things I liked best was the choir outing which was always held at Miss Watson's house. There was good food and singing around the piano. Perhaps there were games – memory falters – but certainly it was a highlight in the school calendar.

When I was in the sixth form I shared a room with Judy Stringer. Judy came from Zanzibar; she was blonde and beautiful and self-possessed and had a much older boyfriend called Mike. One term Mike flew up from Zanzibar to visit Judy. He stayed in the nearby Highlands Hotel and wanted to take Judy out for the evening. Miss Fisher was not having any of it. Goodness knows what Judy might get up to alone in a hotel with a man! Judy was not bypassing such an invitation.

It was the night of the choir outing to Miss Watson's

house. Judy was a leading light in the choir so the plan was that when the choir set off on the school bus, I would explain that Judy had a sudden upset stomach and could not go on the outing. Judy would slip out from the milling group of girls boarding the bus and hide in the bushes. Once the bus had left she would run down the drive and Mike would pick her up at the gate. At the end of the evening, the reverse procedure would take place. I was not confident the plan would work but what are friends for if not to help? The evening came and the first part of the plan worked like a treat. I did not enjoy the party in the usual way and was too nervous to eat much. At 10 o'clock, we boarded the bus for the return journey; the bus turned into the drive and caught in the headlights was the shadow of a figure dropping down behind a large bush on the side of the road. My heart stopped. The bus drew up at the door and disgorged its occupants. As they filed into the school Judy brought up the rear slipping in unnoticed. "I had a fantastic evening," she said as they undressed. "How did the party go?" I vowed I would not be party to Judy's escapades any more. It was too nerve-wracking.

There were other incidents that stand out in school life. A girl we'll call Penny joined the school two years after me. She came from Tanzania. She was a clever girl but never happy. One day I was aware that Penny had been missing from class so I went upstairs to see if she was in the dormitory. To my horror I found Penny trying to cut her wrist with a knife. In the tussle that followed as I tried to take the knife away from her, she bit my thumb. The scar is proof of the truth of this story! Unfortunately, Matron was no help. She herself was having a nervous breakdown. I knocked on her door but when I went in, I found Matron sitting at the window talking nonsense to herself. I was so alarmed that I found Miss Fisher who tracked down Matron sitting on a fallen tree trunk in the school grounds addressing the branches. A car came and she was bundled in never to be seen again.

But there were highlights too. Miss Ford taught history. Before she was dismissed for allegedly having an affair with her house servant, she discovered that I had never been to the cinema. She was so horrified at this lapse in my education that she took me to the cinema in Nairobi to see the musical "Gigi". It was a wonderful evening. The film was full of music, dance and Romance. When we got back to the school Miss Ford gave me a Cornish pasty for my supper. She said it was the only thing she could cook and she certainly knew how to make a memorable pasty! Funnily enough, she looked exactly like a pasty!

And then there was Gordon. He was 5 foot 6 inches, came from the East End of London, was 19 years old and had a crew cut. He was in the army. I was 16 and must have met him when I went to the Nairobi Show. He obviously felt lonely so he started writing to me. Oh, the excitement of receiving letters from a boy – even if I didn't like the boy much. At least I felt attractive enough to have made my mark on somebody. Poor Lad! Somebody was better than nobody. After a few weeks, he asked if he could meet me when I next had a weekend exeat. I was due to go out with the lovely missionary family so I said I would meet him after church on the Sunday. I knew they would be going to the Nairobi Cathedral because they always did. He was there smiling at me from one of the back pews. I got cold feet. At the end of the service, I saw him waiting for me at the back entrance. I slipped out of my seat and hid in one of the side pews – poor Gordon! When Gordon had gone and the search for a missing Rachel had begun, I emerged from my hiding place and told the lovely missionary lady what was going on. She smuggled me out of a side door and into the car. Gordon wrote a sad letter but my foray into romance was enough to last me a long time!

One of the things I really enjoyed at school was acting. One year the end-of-school play was a stage adaptation of "A Christmas Carol". I was cast as Marley's ghost. The part demanded a ghostly scream which I produced so convincingly that some of the juniors were so terrified they had to be reminded it was just make-believe and given reviving mugs of hot chocolate before bedtime. I was a success in the part and longed for my parents to be able to come to the performance open to an audience but the journey was too long – though not too long for them to come up for David's sports day when he won the Victor Ludorum! In missionary eyes, acting was deemed heathen whereas sport was healthy and worth celebrating, a differentiation that didn't occur to me at 16 – I just felt jealous.

Despite my limitations, I did all that was expected of me as house captain including coaching a team for the Scottish dancing competition. To everyone's surprise – mine included – our team won! Eventually, I was able to convince Matron that I was quite capable of managing the stairs to sleep on the top floor in the twin room reserved for senior prefects. I shared the room with glamorous Judy and a large photo of Mike. Listening to Judy talking about her holidays in Zanzibar, where she lived, was like listening to a romantic novel and opened my eyes to a world far removed from the missionary world I inhabited. Judy enjoyed more romantic dinners with Mike but a letter to the headmistress from her parents permitting her to go out with Mike removed the necessity for hiding in the bushes. This was a great relief as my nerves wouldn't stand up to many more adventures!

Miss Fisher left the school leaving as her legacy a beautiful school chapel which was blessed by the Archbishop of Canterbury, Dr Fisher. She became the head of a school in South Africa and then went on to become the head of Wycombe Abbey. She was followed by Miss Cable who was small and round and plain with a pudding-basin haircut and no presence at all. By this time I had become Head of House and was struggling with A levels. I did English, History and Latin as my main subjects with French as a subsidiary. By that time, Miss Ford had been hastily dismissed so I was told to learn what I could from texts to be found in the library. Needless to say, there was no hope of my passing an exam but I was okay in the other subjects.

I filled in for nine months helping at the Kabale school and then went to Homerton. Luckily for me, Aunty Doris was good friends with the Principal of Homerton so I flew back to England in August and went up for an interview with Miss Gage, the Principal. She accepted me. "Do not let me down!" said Miss Gage as she closed the door on me at the end of the interview. I struggled with the whole Cambridge life but I didn't let her down coming out at the end of two years with an honours certificate.

My memories of Cambridge are haphazard. I studied Divinity and drama – though I had enough drama in my life not to need to study it! As did everybody, I had a bike which I cycled all over Cambridge. I became friends with a law student whose home was down the road from my grandparents. It might have been a romance but Anthony Hindley was always in the background. I even went up to Durham where he was studying, for a very happy weekend. But we were both young and my father felt we both should be focussing on our studies so, to my utter disgust, he wrote to both of them forbidding any more contact between them. Can you imagine my fury? For about nine months we obeyed his command then one day we met, accidentally defying parental control.

Before very long Anthony took me out for the day. By

now I had spent my post office savings on a blue Austin 7 car – my pride and joy – so we used the car and went to Coventry to see the Cathedral but we didn't do much Cathedral viewing because Anthony proposed! When we got home he went into the study to ask my father's permission to marry me which, surprisingly, he was willingly given. We went up to London the next day to buy an engagement ring, using the money cousin Betty had given each of the brothers – £100, a fortune in those days. My ring was a beautiful sapphire and two diamond ring so I was very thrilled.

Anthony went back to college in North London, Barnet, and I drove up once a week for a prospective clergy wives' meeting, singularly dull and I didn't conform very well but I did try – well more or less! One evening I scraped the car on one of the bollards driving out in the dark on my way home, leaving a smudge of red paint – the blue Austin had been changed for a red mini by that time; Anthony was too big to be comfortable in the Austin with his legs round his chin! "Have you scraped the car?" was his first question. I denied the accusation hotly accusing the post office van! I went to the garage and bought special sandpaper called "wet and dry" and a pot of red paint and set about my own repair job! So that was that!

We had a big wedding with a marquee in the garden of the house my parents had bought for £15,000 in Bickley near Wendy's parents. It eventually was sold as a home for the staff of the local nursing home and my parents bought a flat in London in the Barbican Centre. My father could walk to Barts Hospital from there where he was the doctor for the nurses and was much loved – wise and compassionate, never too busy for the most junior nurse. When he was 53 he had an aneurysm of the aorta. I flew back from Kenya, where Anthony and I were busy being missionaries, leaving Anthony with three small children and the prospect of moving house which was accomplished with the help of his mother.

I slept on a bed put up in my mother's bedroom in the Barbican flat. Early one morning the phone rang from the hospital to say Daddy had died. Although we had been expecting it, nothing really prepares you for the shock and Mummy's grief-stricken wail will live with me for the rest of my life. All I could feel was gratitude that I had got there in time and had seen him the previous evening. There hadn't been much life in him then but he had at least recognised me. I didn't stay for the funeral – I was needed back home with my own family who was now living in Nakuru. The girl, Mary, who was looking after the children had moved with them all. Mathew, who did all the cooking, stayed on in the house and I was thankful to keep him on – he was an excellent cook and stayed with us for the next nine years while we lived in Nakuru. So I flew back and was very relieved to be reunited with them all.

Here I am in Guildford with Sarah, the next generation

So relieved that Mark was conceived almost immediately! He was born in Nairobi Hospital in the following February, a bonny nine-pound baby who fed well and slept well and was welcomed by his sisters – though his big brother wasn't so sure but had to accept the fact that he had come to stay!

Back in Africa as missionaries with Aunty Gwen and Mark on the way!

By this time Sarah and Annette were both at Turi, a local school filled with all white children – a lot of them missionary offspring joined by white settlers' children, about 150 at a guess. Sarah and Annette were lucky enough to have Aunty Sue, Anthony's older sister, on the staff and she kept a motherly eye on them. As a thank you, we bought Sue a red setter puppy which she named Conker. He became Sue's devoted companion, going into class with her, having to be restrained from taking an active part in games of hockey and providing comfort to lots of homesick children. There are lots of girls and boys who still speak lovingly of Conker.

Eventually, the time came to leave Kenya. Sarah was ready for secondary education and there was no way we were going to repeat their experience of separation during those formative years. So we packed our bags and Anthony got a lift to Nairobi with the Pollards – a farming couple, slightly older and going to Nairobi in an empty car, plenty of room for Anthony. I had a really bad feeling about the trip and begged Anthony not to go but he couldn't see the logic so went. They were involved in a nasty accident on the escarpment. A lorry was on the wrong side of the road and hit them head-on, killing both the Pollards and injuring Anthony who was taken straight to Nairobi hospital. He had a broken hip and head injuries so spent time in hospital there and then was transferred to Nakuru Hospital where at least I could visit him. I packed up the house, sent off household goods, and packed suitcases for us and the children. Once Anthony was well enough to come out of hospital and we flew to England taking with us the two older Williamson children to give them a basic knowledge of England before the family came so that they could help Ruth settle in. At least they would understand English money, supermarket shopping and would be able to help their mother settle in. We went to live in Redhill. The older children went to secondary school and the younger two went to primary school. Education was interrupted when the younger boys got mumps! Mercifully, they recovered quickly but there was a moment when Jonathan asked bravely if it was going to hurt any worse than it did. I answered with an emphatic no – poor child!

With no job and therefore no income, I had to go to the job centre once a week to line up for our benefits and coupons for free school meals – all very humiliating I felt. Money was very tight and one week there simply wasn't enough to feed us all so I raided my jewellery box and took a string of pearls into a jeweller who was happy to buy it for a song but enough to pay the grocery bill. The irony was that the next day, rich cousin Betty sent a rescue cheque. I rushed back to see if I could redeem my pearls but too late – they had been sold! My Aunt was so horrified she sent me a spare string of hers but they weren't a patch on the original string though I am still wearing them. One day I'll replace them with a decent string.

Eventually, the rest of the Williamson family came back from Kenya and took the two children to live with them in Hurstpierpoint where Robin, whom we had known in Kenya, had a flat that went with the job at Hurst College where he was to teach English. Anthony and I were to take over a church in Eastbourne where we were to live in a beautiful, enormous Vicarage. Curtains had to be made so I set to. The drop in the sitting room was 10 feet! Likewise in the dining room. The children settled into new schools. Uncle Raymond paid for the boys to go to St. Andrews Prep School and later on to Eastbourne College. He didn't see the need for girls to have quality education so they went to the local grammar/comprehensive school. Annette drew the short straw as her year was the year that changed from grammar to comprehensive. Sarah was in grammar school. Both girls did well, and went on to university as did the boys. They were happy, settled years.

I got a job in the local sixth form college where my job depended on keeping my register full. As attendance was voluntary, this was no mean feat particularly as there were no course books and I had no idea where to find any. Somehow I muddled through, learning the wisdom of giving my students cigarette breaks and remembering I was teaching adults.

One of my class was a very clever male nurse who needed some GCSEs to put on his CV so found himself in my English class. Both class and teacher were very impressed with his knowledge – one of the students said, "Aren't you scared of trying to teach him when he knows so much more than any of the rest of us?" My reply was, "He may know more but he needs a GCSE in English and my job is to help him get one!" The trouble was he couldn't believe the questions he was being asked were as straightforward as they were so he tended to give far too much information and was in danger of failing. However, all was well and he passed! Attendance remained high and I was employed year after year.

Then Anthony decided he wanted to move so he approached the Bishop, at that time Bishop Ball! He went to Lewes to meet the churchwardens of a church there.

I had a job at Lewes Old Grammar School, an outfit owned and run by the headmaster who had employed me because he "had to have one disabled person on the staff list". Had I known this, I would never have taken the job. He never did value my ability to teach, even insisting I went to his office before the school day started so that he could go over my lessons with me and show me how to teach them properly. Luckily he only had time to fit in one session or they might have come to blows. I taught well, and the results were proof of that. At the same time, I enrolled at Sussex University to do first an Advanced Certificate of Education, and then an MA in Creative Arts – based mainly on autobiographical writing and some extended original work of their own – it could be writing or any original art form. I chose to write a series of short stories for four-to-six-year-olds. Later, after I had been successful in getting my MA, I sent them up to Penguin who sent them back asking me to edit them. I didn't have an agent to advise me and I took that as rejection so I put them in a drawer and there they stayed!

However, I got my degree and with it, a pay rise which the headmaster didn't at all want to pay but a threat to go to the Union did the trick and I got my rise! I was living in a house in

Lewes, with Mark staying for one night a week and the other three popping in. The girls were at university and Jonathan was applying for medical school. Robin and I bought the house on the Common and got married in April 1988. I got a wonderful job teaching English at the Girls School in Burgess Hill, a ten-minute drive from the house. I loved my job teaching English from Year 7 right up to A level. The house on the Common was a real family base. There were weddings, christenings, birthday parties and impromptu gatherings.

Meanwhile, school life became increasingly busy. A partially sighted girl, funded by the state, joined the school and I was asked to be responsible for her which involved a lot of form filling. In recognition of the extra work, I was promoted to Special Needs Coordinator. Most of my responsibility lay with looking after the dyslexic students. I worked closely with the school's counsellor, Pat, even training as a counsellor myself. Pat went on a course where she heard about a new way of helping dyslexic people based on a book by an American man called Ron Davis. The book is called "The Gift of Dyslexia" and is based on the premise that people with dyslexia are predominately picture thinkers – they run a film through their minds rather than a radio broadcast. I read the book and tried out some of his practices with my dyslexic students in school. They were transformative and I was determined to explore these methods more fully. When I saw a training course was taking place in Winchester I asked for permission to attend it. With Pat's support and funded by my wonderfully generous sister-in-law, I went on the course. It opened up a whole new career for me. I used the methods in school and found girls blossomed, finding their dyslexia truly was a gift and not a handicap. If any of my readers are interested, it is worth reading the book, "The Gift of Dyslexia" by Ron Davis and researching a practitioner in your area.

In 1991 I retired. At the farewell assembly, I was given a standing ovation by the whole school. All I could say through my tears was, "Thank you. You have given me far more than I have given you!" I practised as a Davis Practitioner for the next five years with great success and a feeling of fulfilment. I only wish I had known of this method earlier so that I could have been of more help to girls such as Holly Willoughby who was a student at the school.

For my 70th birthday, Robin's daughter, Jane and her family gave me a cat called Jess, to whom I was devoted. In 2020, I had a stroke which left me even weaker on my left side. Robin's son, Andrew, and his partner, Celia, were homeless at that time and they moved in to look after us. I shall always be grateful to them for both their practical help and their love.

We had some wonderful holidays during those years before my stroke. Andrew and Celia looked after the cottage and the cat while we went to stay with Jane in Switzerland, Sarah in Botswana, and Annette in Australia. During that time Sarah met her future husband, Andy, and married him in Botswana. It was a wonderful, colourful ceremony conducted up in the hills in the open air with a local band playing mirembe – instruments like wooden xylophones. Annette's two little girls were bridesmaids, Sarah's father conducted the ceremony and Annette brought the wedding cake on her flight from Australia. The reception was held in a local restaurant. There were lights on the tables and candles in ostrich eggshells. Annette's two little girls and their four-year-old brother were found fast asleep under one of the tables at the end of the dancing!

In time, the cottage became impractical. Andrew and Celia were given flats of their own and I was finding access to the house increasingly difficult. The house with its four bedrooms was expensive to run. Robin was finding it more and more difficult to manage the garden and bring in coal and wood for the fire that provided a modicum of heat. Sadly it was time to downsize, so we sold the cottage and bought a house in Ditchling in a warden-assisted complex for over 55-year-olds. It was all a terrible wrench, even more for Robin than for me. I love having people drop in and being able to watch the world go by. The cat settled in very well until she had problems with her thyroid and turned really nasty, biting me for no apparent reason. The bites had unpleasant side effects causing swelling and a degree of paralysis so, sadly, we had to have her put down. I miss her terribly.

What a rich life I have been privileged to enjoy, it is no wonder I have chosen to call this autobiography "Rainbow Years" – colourful and a reminder that there is no rainbow without the rain first. So it is in life – with the tears are the joys; you can't have one without the other.

Acknowledgements

Special thanks to Robin who patiently stood by while I became increasingly engrossed in writing this.

Thank you to Anthony for our four wonderful children.

Very special thanks to Jacqueline Coleman for her encouragement. Without the endorsement from her that this is worth printing, it would have lain dormant on the computer, so a big thank you, Jacqueline.

And a final thanks to the team at Spiffing Covers who guided me so sensitively. In particular, Abbie Starling for her careful editing.

Printed in Great Britain
by Amazon

37323464R00066